Steve Smith

$270

P9-EGD-458

Stephen Smith

Botany Project 1996

F - Period Com #96

Choice Number 5: <u>A cx of a woody dicot stem at least io years old.   Measure and record the years of growth.</u>

A cross section of a dicot stem is a view of the inside of the stem. Each line circulation the pith (center part of stem) represents one year of gowth. The phloem and camblum are two tissues scattered around the pith. Camblum makes the stem a woody stem. (Mrs. Duffy please help me out on this one I can't find to much more info on it)

Stephen Smith

Botany Project 1996

F Period Com # 96

Choice number 24: <u>A comparison of cross sections of herbaceuous dicot stem and monocot stem cross sections. Obtain stems, soak in dye, section, mount, and identify tissues.</u>

A Herbaceuous (nonwoody) stem is one which has a protective epidermis covering a cortex that consistsmainly of parenchyma (packing tissue) but also has some collenchyma (supporting tissue). Rhe vascular tissue of such stems is arranged in bundles, each of which consists of xylem,phloem, and sclerenchyma (strengthening tissues).

A herbaceuous dicot stem is a nonwoody stem with leaves that are broad with a central midrid and branched veins. Vascular bundles are arranged in a rig around the stem. Dicots can be either woody or herbaceuous depending on if it has cambium(wood producing).

Monocot stem cross section will difer with the dicot one becausw they are two different classes. The monocot leaves will be long and narrowwith parellel veins. Vascular tissues are scattered tissues are scattered in random bundles throughout the stem. Because they lack stem cambium (actively dividing cells that produce wood), most monocot are herbaceuous.

Stephen Smith

Botany Project 1996

F Period - Com. # 96

Choice Number 33: <u>Three different varieties of Quercus complete with leaf, stem, buds, and optimally seeds.</u>

Quercus is the scientific name for Oak. Of all the broad leaved trees in North America, Oaks are the widespred, have the greatest variety of habitats, and comprimise the greatest number of species. Pinpointing the species of Oak is easiest if the tree is first classified in to one of the two groups - the red oaks or white oaks. Red Oaks bear tiny bristles at the tip of the leaf, at the ends of the lobes, or both. Their bittter acorns require two years to mature, (they therefore remain on the trees in winter) and wooly hair line the cup. The leavesof the white Oaks have rounded lobes devoid of bristles. Their sweet acorn mature in six months and the acorns are gone by winter. The individual species of Oak can be identified from their leaves, fruits, and acrons.

Both red oak and white oak are can be found in the northeast. For example Red Oak there is , Scarlet Oak(in dry sandy to gravelly soils), Pin OAk(in wet bottomlands), and Northern Red Oak (found in bottomlands, slopes, and uplands on well drained loam). The White Oak species that can be found in New England include White Oak (found in riverbanks, moist valleys to sandy plains, and dry hillsides), Post Oak (dry sandy uplands and plains, rocky ridges and hills; river banks and loams), Chestnut Oak (habitat of dry sandy uplands to rocky ridges; valleys with wel drained soil.

Stephen Smith

Botany Project 1996

F - Period - com #96

Choice Number 32: <u>A sample of a xerophile and a acidophile.</u>

Xerophile (xerophytes) is a plant that is able to survive in unfavorable habitats. All are found in dry areas and somelive in high temperatures that cause excessive loss of water from leaves. They show a number of adaptaions to dry conditions like reduced leaf area, rolled leaves, sunken stomata, hairs, spines, and thick cuticles. They store water in especially large roots, leaves, and stems. Cacti is a good example of a xerophyte. It has stems that are fleshy, green, and photosynthetic. They are typically ribbed or covered intubercles in rows, with leaves being reduced to spines or entirely absent.

Acidophile (acidophytes) are plants in marshy areas or in or near water. They show many adaptions to their habitat. Typically there are numrous gas spaces inside the stems, leaves an roots; these aid gas exchange and buoyancy. Subermerged parts of the plant generally have no cuticle (waterproof covering) allowing plants to absorb minerals and gases directly from the water.   Because they are supported by water, wetland plants need little of the suportive tissue found in land plants. Stomata, the gas exchange pores, aren't in plants that are completely submerged in water. Most acidophytes have rhizomes instead of roots that get the nutrients it needs from the water.

Stephen Smith

Botany Project 1996

F - period Com #96

Choice Number 6: <u>Three different types of fruits that have been found in natural</u>

<u>enviroments.</u>

The most common fruit to find around here this season are the dry fruits. Dry

fruits have a dry pericarp (fruit wall) around their seeds. There are three types of

dryfruits dehiscent, in which the pericarp splits open to release the seeds; indehiscent,

which do not split open; and schizocarpic in which fruit splits but he seeds are not

exposed. Dehiscent dry fruits include capsules, follicles, legumes (pea) and siliqiuas

(honesty). Sees of these types are dipersed by the wind. Indehiscent fruits include

nuts (sweet chestnut) , nutlets, strawberry, wheat, elm, and dandelion. These seeds

are dispersed by the wind and help by things on the seeds themselves such as wings.

Schizocarpics include hogweed and sycamore and are dipsersed by the wind.

THE VISUAL
DICTIONARY *of*
PLANTS

*Spadix
(fleshy axis
carrying male
and female flowers)*

*Spathe
(large bract)*

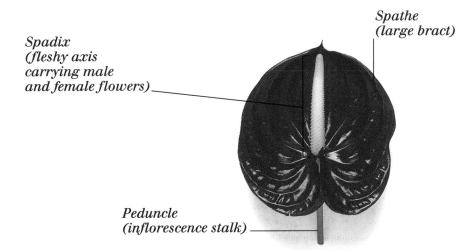

*Peduncle
(inflorescence stalk)*

PAINTER'S PALETTE
(*Anthurium andreanum*)

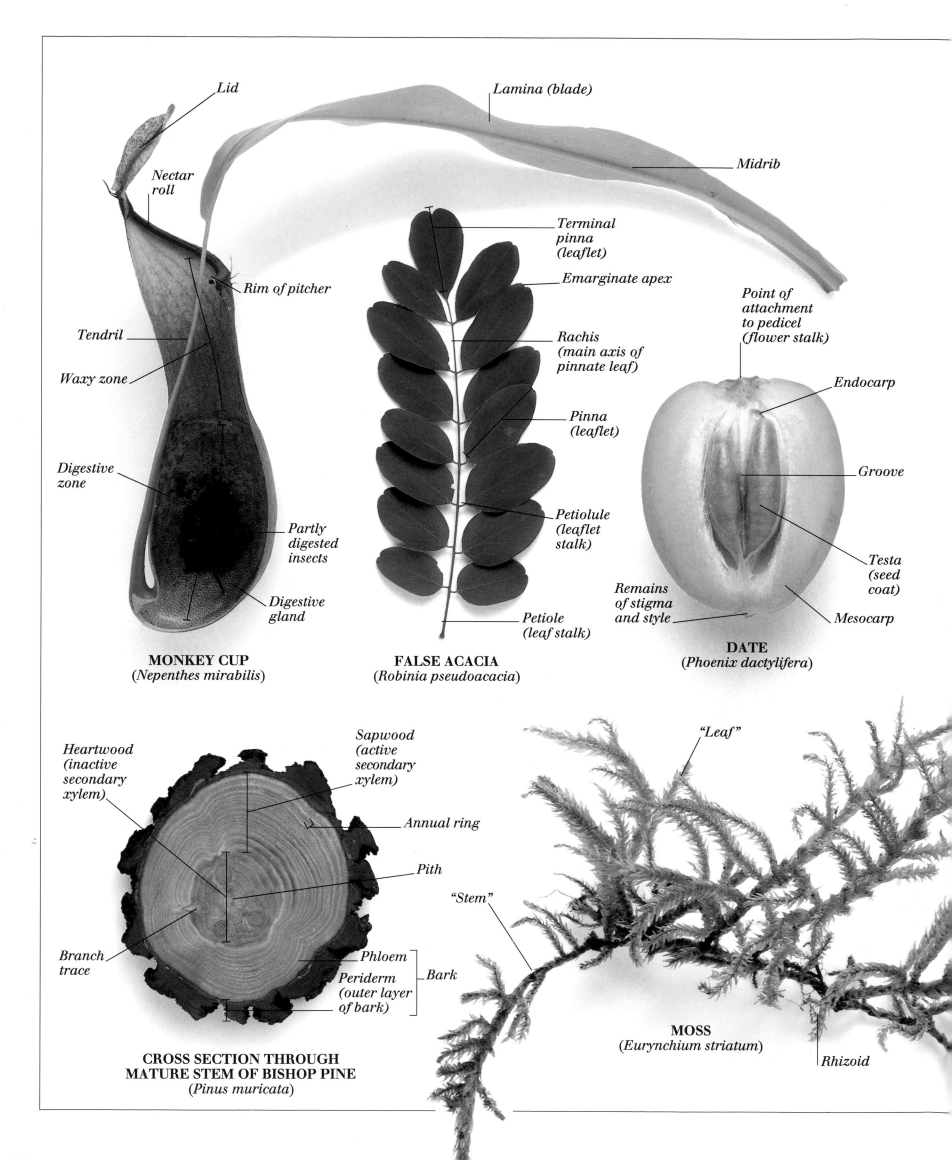

Lid

Lamina (blade)

Midrib

Nectar
roll

Rim of pitcher

Tendril

Waxy zone

Digestive
zone

Partly
digested
insects

Digestive
gland

Terminal
pinna
(leaflet)

Emarginate apex

Rachis
(main axis of
pinnate leaf)

Pinna
(leaflet)

Petiolule
(leaflet
stalk)

Petiole
(leaf stalk)

Point of
attachment
to pedicel
(flower stalk)

Endocarp

Groove

Testa
(seed
coat)

Mesocarp

Remains
of stigma
and style

MONKEY CUP
(*Nepenthes mirabilis*)

FALSE ACACIA
(*Robinia pseudoacacia*)

DATE
(*Phoenix dactylifera*)

Heartwood
(inactive
secondary
xylem)

Sapwood
(active
secondary
xylem)

Annual ring

Pith

Branch
trace

Phloem

Periderm
(outer layer
of bark)

Bark

"Leaf"

"Stem"

**CROSS SECTION THROUGH
MATURE STEM OF BISHOP PINE**
(*Pinus muricata*)

MOSS
(*Eurynchium striatum*)

Rhizoid

EYEWITNESS VISUAL DICTIONARIES

THE VISUAL
DICTIONARY *of*
PLANTS

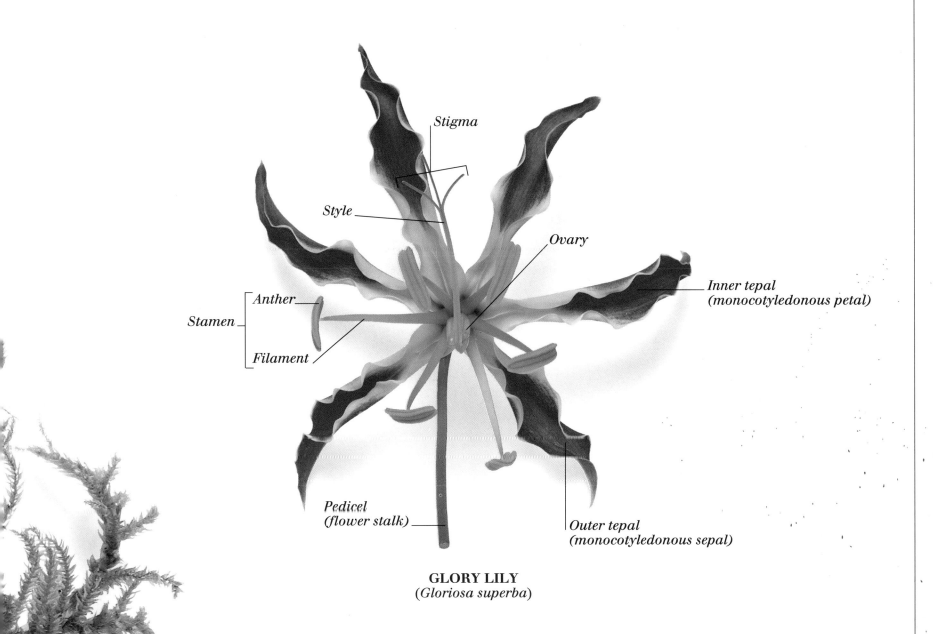

Stigma

Style

Ovary

Inner tepal
(monocotyledonous petal)

Anther

Stamen

Filament

Pedicel
(flower stalk)

Outer tepal
(monocotyledonous sepal)

GLORY LILY
(*Gloriosa superba*)

DORLING KINDERSLEY, INC.

NEW YORK

A DORLING KINDERSLEY BOOK

Project Art Editor Bryn Walls
Designer Andrew Nash

Project Editor Mary Lindsay
Consultant Editor Dr. Richard Walker
U.S. Editor Charles Wills

Series Art Editor Stephen Knowlden
Series Editor Martyn Page
Art Director Chez Picthall
Managing Editor Ruth Midgley

Photography Peter Chadwick, Geoff Dann, Natural History Museum, Spike Walker
Illustrations Simone End, John Woodcock
Production Hilary Stephens

Botanical Models Supplied By Somso Modelle, Coburg, Germany

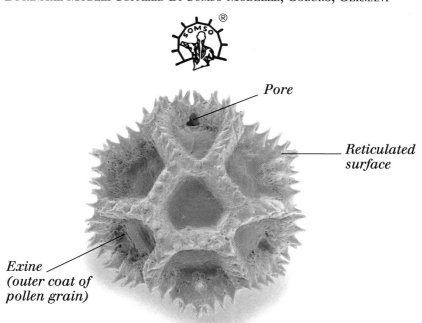

Pore

Reticulated surface

Exine
(outer coat of
pollen grain)

MICROGRAPH OF POLLEN GRAIN

First American Edition, 1992
10 9 8 7 6 5 4 3 2 1

Dorling Kindersley, Inc., 232 Madison Avenue
New York, New York 10016

Copyright © 1992 Dorling Kindersley Limited, London

All rights reserved under International and Pan-American Copyright Conventions.
Published in the United States by Dorling Kindersley, Inc., New York, New York.
Distributed by Houghton Mifflin Company, Boston, Massachusetts.
Published in Great Britain by Dorling Kindersley Limited, London.
No part of this publication may be reproduced, stored in a retrieval system,
or transmitted in any form or by any means, electronic, mechanical, photocopying, recording
or otherwise, without the prior written permission of the copyright owner.

Library of Congress Cataloging-in-Publication Data
Eyewitness visual dictionary of plants.   1st American ed.
p. cm. — (The Eyewitness visual dictionaries)
Includes index.
Summary: Text and labeled illustrations depict a variety of plants
and their parts, including woody, flowering, desert, and tropical plants.
ISBN 1–56458–016–4 — ISBN 1–56458–017–2
1. Plants—Terminology—Juvenile literature. 2. Plants—Pictorial works—Juvenile literature.
3. Picture dictionaries, English—Juvenile literature. [1. Plants] I. Dorling Kindersley, Inc.
II. Series.
QK49.E94 1992
581—dc20
91–58208
CIP
AC

Reproduced by Colourscan, Singapore
Printed and bound by Arnoldo Mondadori, Verona, Italy

Exocarp (outer layer of pericarp)

Remains of style

Drupelet

Remains of stamen

Remains of sepal

Pedicel (flower stalk)

BLACKBERRY
(Rubus fruticosus)

Vein

Midrib

Petiole (leaf stalk)

CHECKERBLOOM
(Sidalcea malviflora)

Contents

Tree bark

Soredia (vegetative fragments) produced at end of lobe

Lobe

Foliose (leafy) thallus

LICHEN
(Hypogymnia physodes)

Woody ovuliferous scale

Female cone

BHUTAN PINE
(Pinus wallichiana)

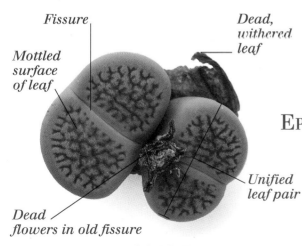

Fissure

Mottled surface of leaf

Dead, withered leaf

Dead flowers in old fissure

Unified leaf pair

LIVING STONE
(Lithops bromfieldii)

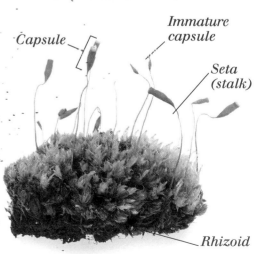

Capsule

Immature capsule

Seta (stalk)

Rhizoid

MOSS
(Bryum Sp.)

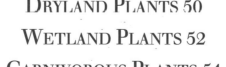

Plant varieties

THERE ARE MORE THAN 300,000 SPECIES of plants. They
show a wide diversity of forms, ranging from delicate liverworts, adapted for life
in a damp habitat, to cacti, capable of surviving in the desert. The plant kingdom includes
herbaceous plants, such as corn, which completes its life cycle in one year, to the giant redwood tree, which
can live for thousands of years. This diversity reflects the adaptations of plants to survive in a wide range of
habitats. This is seen most clearly in the flowering plants (phylum Angiospermophyta), which are the most
numerous, with over 250,000 species. They are also the most widespread, being found from the tropics to the
arctic. Despite their diversity, plants share certain characteristics. Typically, plants are green, and make their
food by photosynthesis. Most plants live in or on a substrate, such as soil, and do not actively move. Algae
(kingdom Protista) and fungi (kingdom Fungi) have some plantlike characteristics and are
often studied alongside plants, although they are not true plants.

FLOWERING PLANT
Bromeliad
(*Acanthostachys strobilacea*)

Leaf

GREEN ALGA
Micrograph of desmid
(*Micrasterias sp.*)

FERN
Tree fern
(*Dicksonia antarctica*)

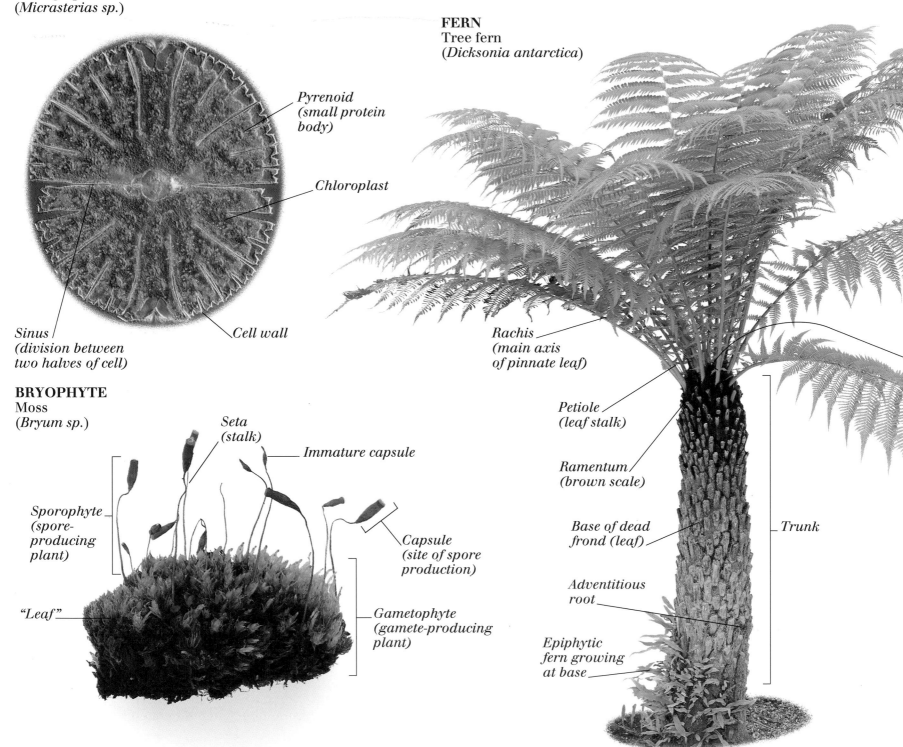

Pyrenoid
(*small protein
body*)

Chloroplast

Sinus
(*division between
two halves of cell*)

Cell wall

Rachis
(*main axis
of pinnate leaf*)

Petiole
(*leaf stalk*)

Ramentum
(*brown scale*)

BRYOPHYTE
Moss
(*Bryum sp.*)

Seta
(*stalk*)

Immature capsule

Sporophyte
(*spore-
producing
plant*)

Capsule
(*site of spore
production*)

"Leaf"

Gametophyte
(*gamete-producing
plant*)

Base of dead
frond (leaf)

Trunk

Adventitious
root

Epiphytic
fern growing
at base

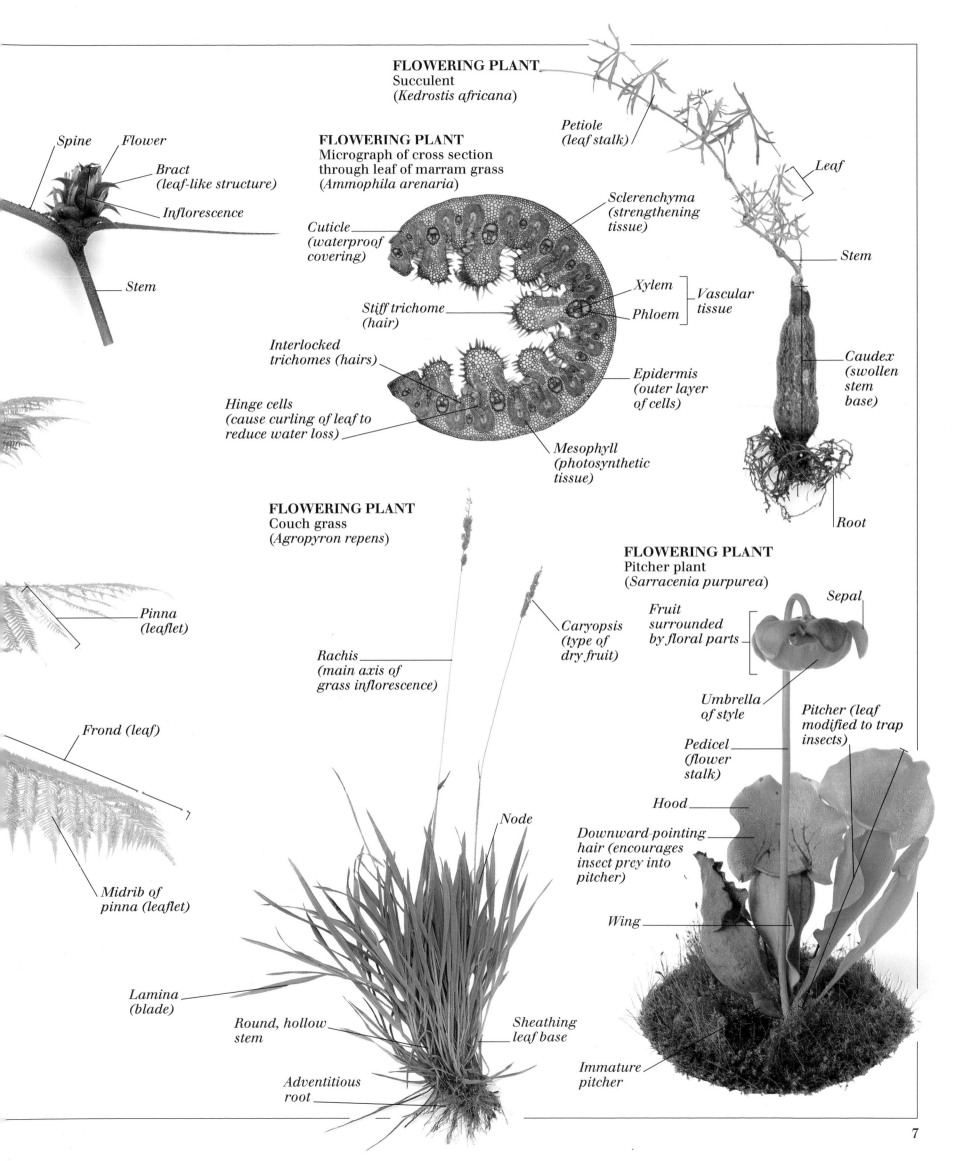

FLOWERING PLANT
Succulent
(*Kedrostis africana*)

Spine

Flower

Bract
(leaf-like structure)

Inflorescence

Stem

FLOWERING PLANT
Micrograph of cross section
through leaf of marram grass
(*Ammophila arenaria*)

Petiole
(leaf stalk)

Leaf

Sclerenchyma
(strengthening
tissue)

Cuticle
(waterproof
covering)

Stem

Xylem

Vascular
tissue

Phloem

Stiff trichome
(hair)

Caudex
(swollen
stem
base)

Interlocked
trichomes (hairs)

Epidermis
(outer layer
of cells)

Hinge cells
(cause curling of leaf to
reduce water loss)

Mesophyll
(photosynthetic
tissue)

Root

FLOWERING PLANT
Couch grass
(*Agropyron repens*)

FLOWERING PLANT
Pitcher plant
(*Sarracenia purpurea*)

Pinna
(leaflet)

Sepal

Fruit
surrounded
by floral parts

Caryopsis
(type of
dry fruit)

Rachis
(main axis of
grass inflorescence)

Frond (leaf)

Umbrella
of style

Pitcher (leaf
modified to trap
insects)

Pedicel
(flower
stalk)

Hood

Node

Downward-pointing
hair (encourages
insect prey into
pitcher)

Midrib of
pinna (leaflet)

Wing

Lamina
(blade)

Round, hollow
stem

Sheathing
leaf base

Adventitious
root

Immature
pitcher

Fungi and lichens

FUNGI WERE ONCE THOUGHT OF AS PLANTS but are now classified as a separate kingdom. This kingdom includes not only the familiar mushrooms, puffballs, stinkhorns, and molds, but also yeasts, smuts, rusts, and lichens. Most fungi are multicellular, consisting of a mass of thread-like hyphae that together form a mycelium. However, the simpler fungi, like yeasts, are microscopic, single-celled organisms. Typically, fungi reproduce by means of spores. Most fungi feed on dead or decaying matter or on living organisms. A few fungi obtain their food from plants or algae, with which they have a symbiotic (mutually advantageous) relationship. Lichens are a symbiotic partnership between algae and fungi. Of the six types of lichens the three most common are crustose (flat and crusty), foliose (leafy), and fruticose (shrub-like). Some lichens (such as *Cladonia floerkeana*) are a combination of types. Lichens reproduce by means of spores or soredia (powdery vegetative fragments).

EXAMPLES OF FUNGI

Emerging sporophore (spore-bearing structure)

Pileus (cap) continuous with stipe (stalk)

Bark of dead beech tree

Inrolled margin of pileus (cap)

Gill (site of spore production)

Sporophore (spore-bearing structure)

Stipe (stalk)

Hyphae (fungal filaments)

OYSTER FUNGUS
(*Pleurotus pulmonarius*)

EXAMPLES OF LICHENS

Secondary fruticose thallus

Branched, hollow stem

Apothecium (spore-producing body)

FRUTICOSE
Cladonia portentosa

Soredia (powdery vegetative fragments) produced at end of lobe

Tree bark

Foliose thallus

FOLIOSE
Hypogymnia physodes

Soredia (powdery vegetative fragments) released onto surface of squamulose thallus

Apothecium (spore-producing body)

Basal scale of primary squamulose thallus

Moss

Podetium (granular stalk) of secondary fruticose thallus

SQUAMULOSE (SCALY) AND FRUTICOSE THALLUS
Cladonia floerkeana

Gleba (spore-producing tissue found in this type of fungus)

Sporophore (spore-bearing structure)

Porous stipe (stalk)

Volva (remains of universal veil)

STINKHORN
(*Phallus impudicus*)

Toothed branchlet

Branch

Sporophore (spore-bearing structure)

Stipe (stalk)

RAMARIA FORMOSA

SECTION THROUGH FOLIOSE LICHEN SHOWING REPRODUCTION BY SOREDIA

Soredium (powdery vegetative fragment involved in propagation) released from lichen

Algal cell

Fungal hypha

Upper cortex

Algal layer

Medulla of fungal hyphae (mycelium)

Lower cortex

Rhizine (bundle of absorptive hyphae)

Soralium (pore in upper surface of thallus)

Upper surface of thallus

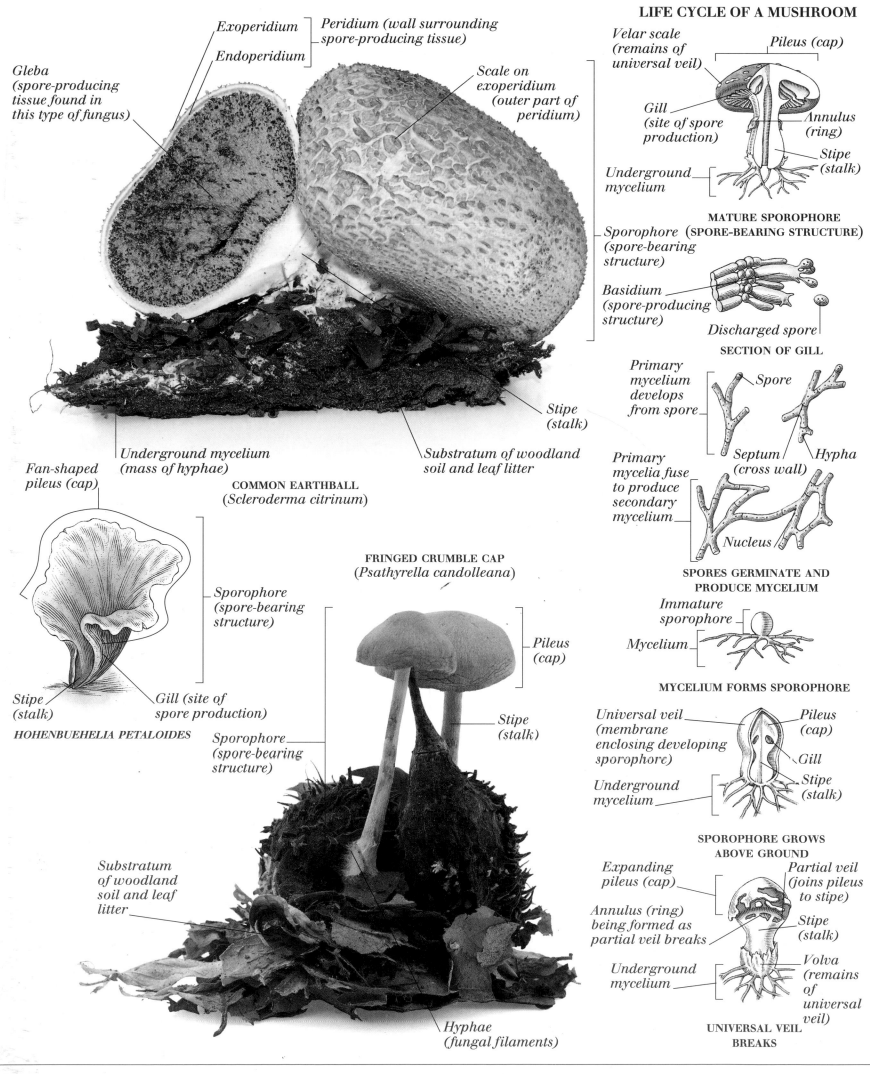

Gleba
(spore-producing
tissue found in
this type of fungus)

Exoperidium

Endoperidium

Peridium (wall surrounding
spore-producing tissue)

Scale on
exoperidium
(outer part of
peridium)

Underground mycelium
(mass of hyphae)

Stipe
(stalk)

Substratum of woodland
soil and leaf litter

COMMON EARTHBALL
(*Scleroderma citrinum*)

Fan-shaped
pileus (cap)

Sporophore
(spore-bearing
structure)

Stipe
(stalk)

Gill (site of
spore production)

HOHENBUEHELIA PETALOIDES

FRINGED CRUMBLE CAP
(*Psathyrella candolleana*)

Sporophore
(spore-bearing
structure)

Pileus
(cap)

Stipe
(stalk)

Substratum
of woodland
soil and leaf
litter

Hyphae
(fungal filaments)

LIFE CYCLE OF A MUSHROOM

Velar scale
(remains of
universal veil)

Pileus (cap)

Gill
(site of spore
production)

Annulus
(ring)

Underground
mycelium

Stipe
(stalk)

MATURE SPOROPHORE

Sporophore (SPORE-BEARING STRUCTURE)
(spore-bearing
structure)

Basidium
(spore-producing
structure)

Discharged spore

SECTION OF GILL

Primary
mycelium
develops
from spore

Spore

Primary
mycelia fuse
to produce
secondary
mycelium

Septum
(cross wall)

Hypha

Nucleus

**SPORES GERMINATE AND
PRODUCE MYCELIUM**

Immature
sporophore

Mycelium

MYCELIUM FORMS SPOROPHORE

Universal veil
(membrane
enclosing developing
sporophore)

Pileus
(cap)

Gill

Underground
mycelium

Stipe
(stalk)

**SPOROPHORE GROWS
ABOVE GROUND**

Expanding
pileus (cap)

Partial veil
(joins pileus
to stipe)

Annulus (ring)
being formed as
partial veil breaks

Stipe
(stalk)

Underground
mycelium

Volva
(remains
of
universal
veil)

**UNIVERSAL VEIL
BREAKS**

9

Algae and seaweed

ALGAE ARE NOT TRUE PLANTS. They form a diverse group of plantlike organisms that belong to the kingdom Protista (see p. 58). Like plants, algae possess the green pigment chlorophyll and make their own food by photosynthesis (see pp. 32-33). Many algae also possess other pigments by which they can be classified. For example, the brown pigment fucoxanthin is found in brown algae. Some of the ten phyla of algae are exclusively unicellular (single-celled); others also contain aggregates of cells in filaments or colonies. Three phyla—the Chlorophyta (green algae), Rhodophyta (red algae), and Phaeophyta (brown algae)—contain larger, multicellular, thalloid (flat), marine organisms commonly known as seaweed.

Most algae can reproduce sexually. For example, in brown seaweed *Fucus vesiculosus*, gametes (sex cells) are produced in conceptacles (chambers) in the receptacles (fertile tips of fronds); after their release into the sea, antherozoids (male gametes) and oospheres (female gametes) fuse. The resulting zygote settles on a rock and develops into a new seaweed.

BROWN SEAWEED
Channeled wrack
(*Pelvetia canaliculata*)

Thallus (plant body)

Margin of lamina (blade) rolled inwards to form channel

Receptacle (fertile tip of frond)

Apical notch

Hapteron (holdfast)

BROWN SEAWEED
Spiral wrack
(*Fucus spiralis*)

Apical notch

Conceptacle (chamber)

Receptacle (fertile tip of frond)

Lamina (blade)

Smooth margin

Midrib

Thallus (plant body)

Hapteron (holdfast)

EXAMPLES OF ALGAE

Reproductive chamber

Cap

Sterile whorl

Cell wall

Stalk

Rhizoid

GREEN ALGA
Acetabularia sp.

Flagellum

Eyespot

Contractile vacuole

Cytoplasm

Nucleus

Cell wall

Chloroplast

Pyrenoid (small protein body)

Starch grain

GREEN ALGA
Chlamydomonas sp.

Coenobium (colony of cells)

Daughter coenobium

Girdle

Gelatinous sheath

Nucleus

Biflagellate cell

GREEN ALGA
Volvox sp.

Spine

Cytoplasm

Vacuole

Plastid (photosynthetic organelle)

Nucleus

DIATOM
Thalassiosira sp.

Apical notch

Receptacle (fertile tip of frond)

Conceptacle (chamber) containing reproductive structures

Lamina (blade)

Midrib

RECEPTACLE
Spiral wrack
(*Fucus spiralis*)

BROWN SEAWEED
Oarweed
(*Laminaria digitata*)

Thallus (plant body)

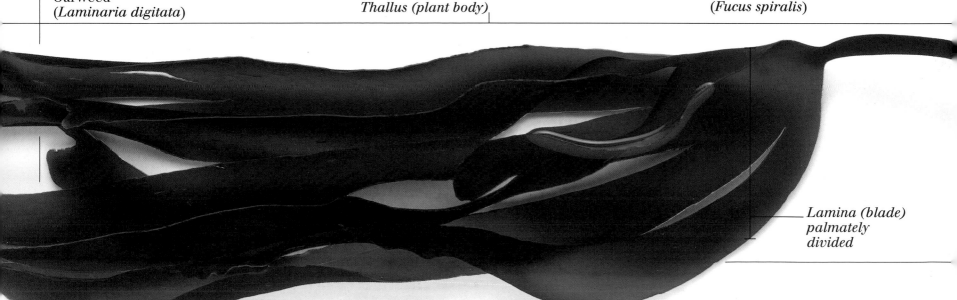

Lamina (blade) palmately divided

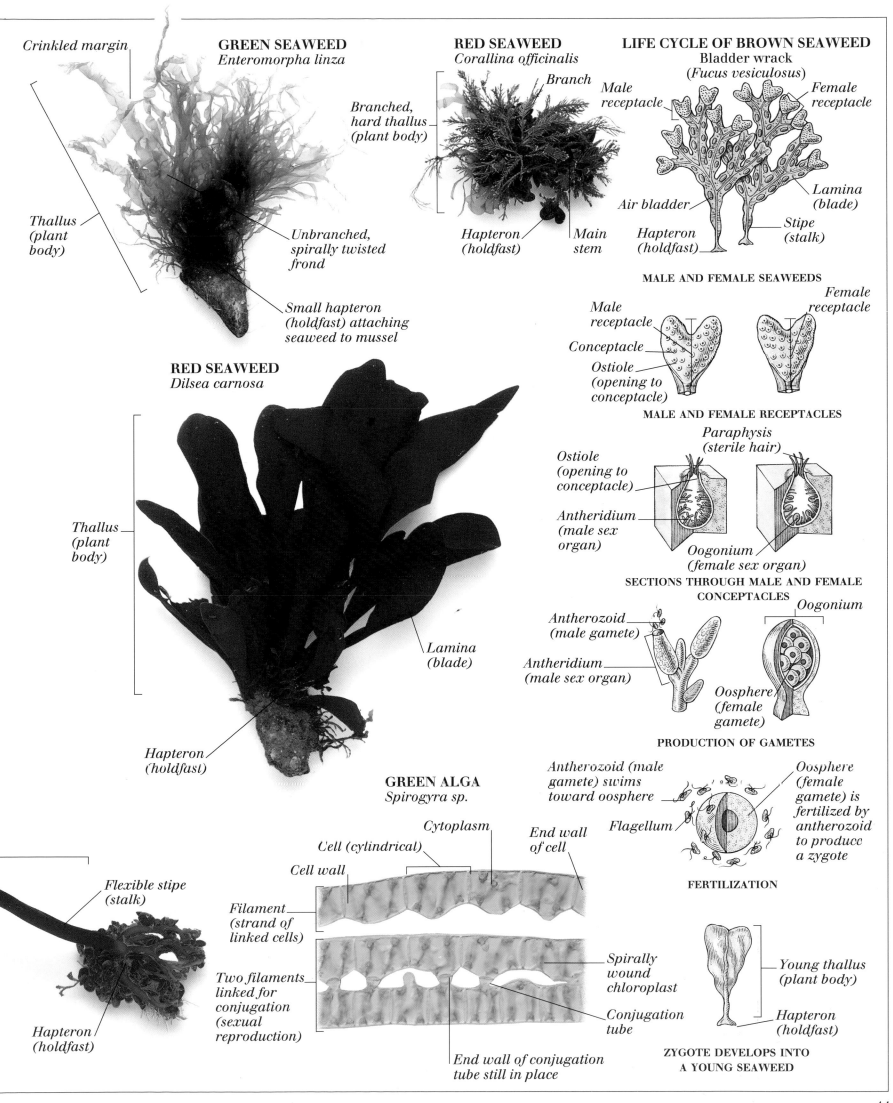

GREEN SEAWEED
Enteromorpha linza

Crinkled margin

Thallus (plant body)

Unbranched, spirally twisted frond

Small hapteron (holdfast) attaching seaweed to mussel

RED SEAWEED
Corallina officinalis

Branch

Branched, hard thallus (plant body)

Hapteron (holdfast)

Main stem

RED SEAWEED
Dilsea carnosa

Thallus (plant body)

Lamina (blade)

Hapteron (holdfast)

Flexible stipe (stalk)

Hapteron (holdfast)

GREEN ALGA
Spirogyra sp.

Cytoplasm

Cell (cylindrical)

Cell wall

End wall of cell

Filament (strand of linked cells)

Two filaments linked for conjugation (sexual reproduction)

Spirally wound chloroplast

Conjugation tube

End wall of conjugation tube still in place

LIFE CYCLE OF BROWN SEAWEED
Bladder wrack
(*Fucus vesiculosus*)

Male receptacle

Female receptacle

Air bladder

Lamina (blade)

Hapteron (holdfast)

Stipe (stalk)

MALE AND FEMALE SEAWEEDS

Male receptacle

Female receptacle

Conceptacle

Ostiole (opening to conceptacle)

MALE AND FEMALE RECEPTACLES

Paraphysis (sterile hair)

Ostiole (opening to conceptacle)

Antheridium (male sex organ)

Oogonium (female sex organ)

SECTIONS THROUGH MALE AND FEMALE CONCEPTACLES

Antherozoid (male gamete)

Oogonium

Antheridium (male sex organ)

Oosphere (female gamete)

PRODUCTION OF GAMETES

Antherozoid (male gamete) swims toward oosphere

Oosphere (female gamete) is fertilized by antherozoid to produce a zygote

Flagellum

FERTILIZATION

Young thallus (plant body)

Hapteron (holdfast)

ZYGOTE DEVELOPS INTO A YOUNG SEAWEED

11

Liverworts and mosses

LIVERWORTS AND MOSSES ARE SMALL, LOW-GROWING PLANTS that belong to the phylum Bryophyta. Bryophytes do not have true stems, leaves, or roots (they are anchored to the ground by rhizoids), nor do they have the vascular tissues (xylem and phloem) that transport water and nutrients in higher plants. With no outer, waterproof cuticle, bryophytes are susceptible to dehydration, and most grow in moist habitats. The bryophyte life cycle has two stages. In stage one, the green plant (gametophyte) produces male and female gametes (sex cells), which fuse to form a zygote. In stage two, the zygote develops into a sporophyte that remains attached to the gametophyte. The sporophyte produces spores, which are released and germinate into new green plants. Liverworts (class Hepaticae) grow horizontally and may be thalloid (flat and ribbon-like) or "leafy." Mosses (class Musci) typically have an upright "stem" with spirally arranged "leaves."

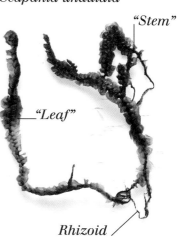

A LEAFY LIVERWORT
Scapania undulata

"Stem"

"Leaf"

Rhizoid

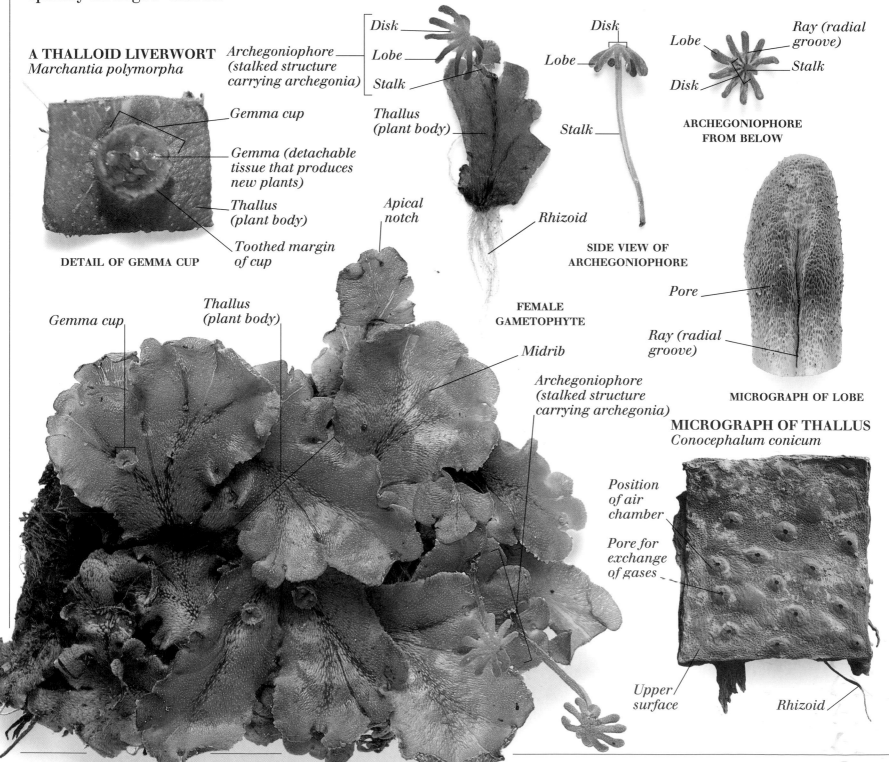

A THALLOID LIVERWORT
Marchantia polymorpha

Gemma cup

Gemma (detachable tissue that produces new plants)

Thallus (plant body)

Toothed margin of cup

DETAIL OF GEMMA CUP

Archegoniophore (stalked structure carrying archegonia)

Disk

Lobe

Stalk

Thallus (plant body)

Apical notch

Rhizoid

FEMALE GAMETOPHYTE

Disk

Lobe

Stalk

SIDE VIEW OF ARCHEGONIOPHORE

Lobe

Disk

Ray (radial groove)

Stalk

ARCHEGONIOPHORE FROM BELOW

Pore

Ray (radial groove)

MICROGRAPH OF LOBE

Gemma cup

Thallus (plant body)

Midrib

Archegoniophore (stalked structure carrying archegonia)

MICROGRAPH OF THALLUS
Conocephalum conicum

Position of air chamber

Pore for exchange of gases

Upper surface

Rhizoid

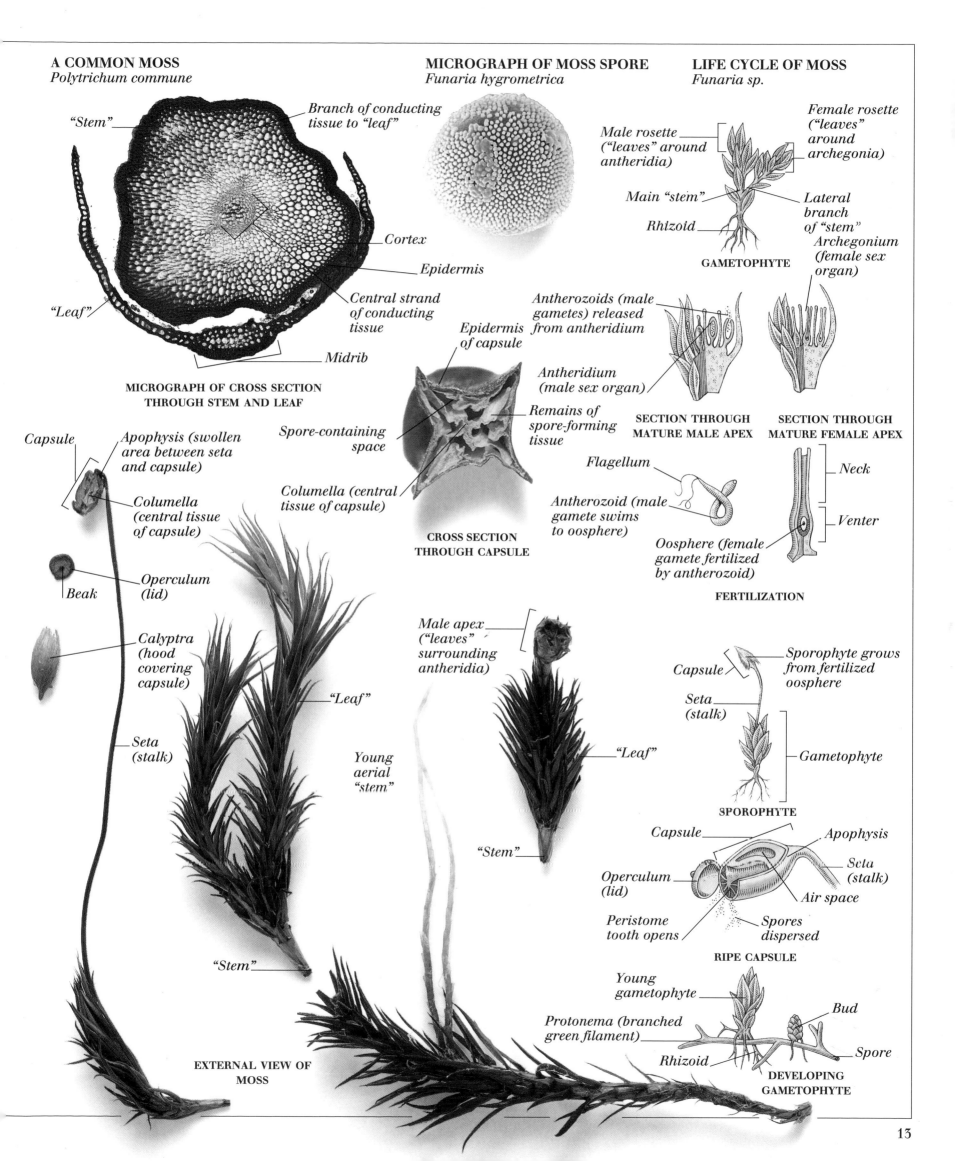

A COMMON MOSS
Polytrichum commune

"Stem"

Branch of conducting
tissue to "leaf"

Cortex

Epidermis

"Leaf"

Central strand
of conducting
tissue

Midrib

**MICROGRAPH OF CROSS SECTION
THROUGH STEM AND LEAF**

Capsule

Apophysis (swollen
area between seta
and capsule)

Columella
(central tissue
of capsule)

Beak

Operculum
(lid)

Calyptra
(hood
covering
capsule)

"Leaf"

Seta
(stalk)

Young
aerial
"stem"

"Stem"

"Stem"

**EXTERNAL VIEW OF
MOSS**

MICROGRAPH OF MOSS SPORE
Funaria hygrometrica

Epidermis
of capsule

Spore-containing
space

Remains of
spore-forming
tissue

Columella (central
tissue of capsule)

**CROSS SECTION
THROUGH CAPSULE**

Male apex
("leaves"
surrounding
antheridia)

"Leaf"

"Stem"

LIFE CYCLE OF MOSS
Funaria sp.

Male rosette
("leaves" around
antheridia)

Female rosette
("leaves"
around
archegonia)

Main "stem"

Rhizoid

Lateral
branch
of "stem"

Archegonium
(female sex
organ)

GAMETOPHYTE

Antherozoids (male
gametes) released
from antheridium

Antheridium
(male sex organ)

**SECTION THROUGH
MATURE MALE APEX**

**SECTION THROUGH
MATURE FEMALE APEX**

Flagellum

Antherozoid (male
gamete swims
to oosphere)

Oosphere (female
gamete fertilized
by antherozoid)

Neck

Venter

FERTILIZATION

Capsule

Seta
(stalk)

Sporophyte grows
from fertilized
oosphere

Gametophyte

SPOROPHYTE

Capsule

Operculum
(lid)

Peristome
tooth opens

Apophysis

Seta
(stalk)

Air space

Spores
dispersed

RIPE CAPSULE

Young
gametophyte

Protonema (branched
green filament)

Rhizoid

Bud

Spore

**DEVELOPING
GAMETOPHYTE**

Horsetails, club mosses, and ferns

HORSETAILS, CLUB MOSSES, AND FERNS are primitive land plants, which, like higher plants, have stems, roots, leaves, and vascular systems that transport water, minerals, and food. Unlike higher plants, however, they do not produce seeds when reproducing. Their life cycles involve two stages. In stage one, the sporophyte (green plant) produces spores in sporangia. In stage two, the spores germinate, developing into small, short-lived gametophyte plants that produce male and female gametes (sex cells). The gametes fuse to form a zygote from which a new sporophyte plant develops. Horsetails (phylum Sphenophyta) have erect green stems with branches arranged in whorls. Some stems are fertile and have a single spore-producing strobilus (group of sporangia) at the tip. Club mosses (phylum Lycopodophyta) typically have small leaves arranged spirally around the stem, with spore-producing strobili at the tip of some stems. Ferns (phylum Filicinophyta) usually have large, pinnate leaves called fronds. Sporangia, grouped together in sori, develop on the underside of fertile fronds.

FROND
Male fern
(*Dryopteris filix-mas*)

CLUB MOSS
Lycopodium sp.

Stem with spirally arranged leaves

Branch

Strobilus (group of sporangia)

CLUB MOSS
Selaginella sp.

Epidermis (outer layer of cells)

Cortex (layer between epidermis and vascular tissue)

Vascular tissue
Phloem
Xylem

Lacuna (air space)

Root

Shoot apex

Branch

Rhizophore (leafless branch)

Creeping stem with spirally arranged leaves

MICROGRAPH OF CROSS SECTION THROUGH CLUB MOSS STEM

HORSETAIL
Common horsetail
(*Equisetum arvense*)

Apex of sterile shoot

Sporangiophore (structure carrying sporangia)

Strobilus (group of sporangia)

Non-photosynthetic fertile stem

Collar of small brown leaves

Young shoot

Lateral branch

Photosynthetic sterile stem

Node

Internode

Node

Tuber

Rhizome

Adventitious root

Endodermis (inner layer of cortex)

Vascular tissue

Sclerenchyma (strengthening tissue)

Epidermis (outer layer of cells)

Chlorenchyma (photosynthetic tissue)

Cortex (layer between epidermis and vascular tissue)

Parenchyma (packing tissue)

Hollow pith cavity

Vallecular canal (longitudinal channel)

Carinal canal (longitudinal channel)

MICROGRAPH OF CROSS SECTION THROUGH HORSETAIL STEM

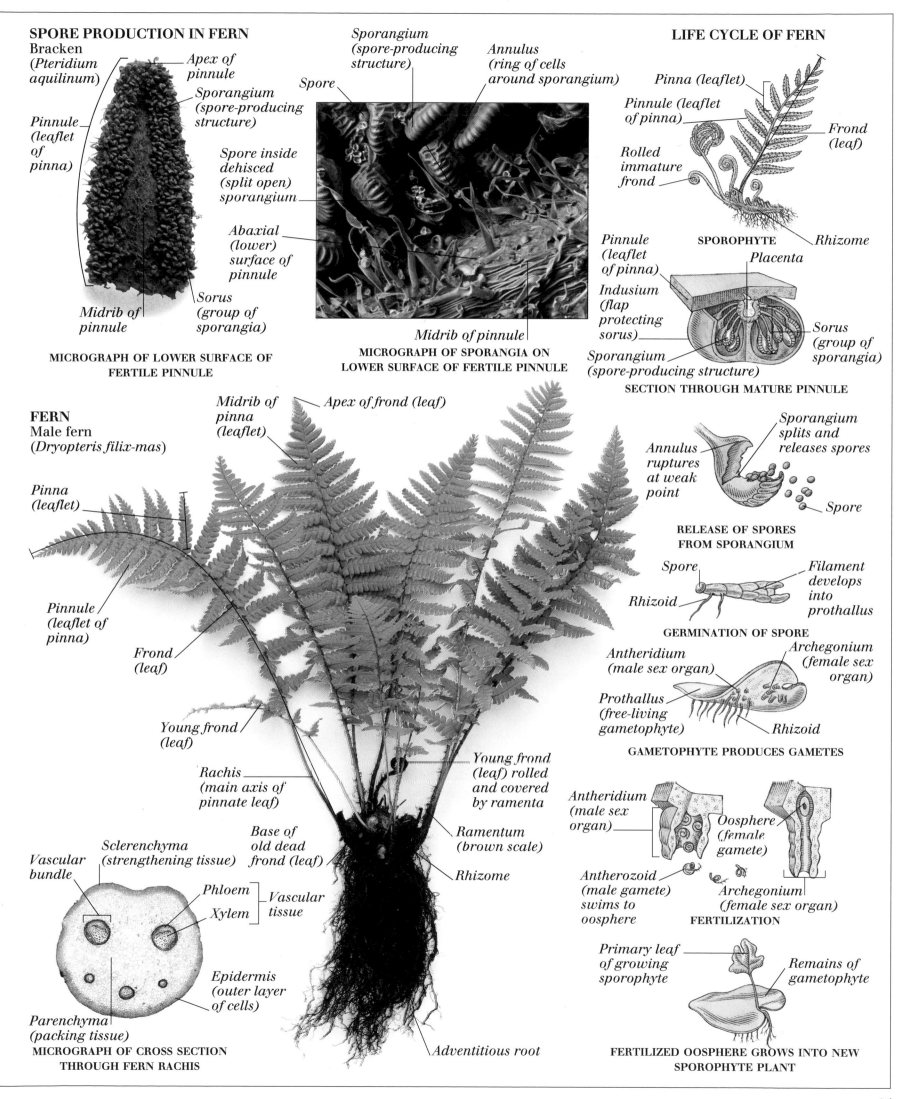

SPORE PRODUCTION IN FERN
Bracken
(*Pteridium aquilinum*)

Apex of pinnule

Pinnule (leaflet of pinna)

Sporangium (spore-producing structure)

Spore

Sporangium (spore-producing structure)

Annulus (ring of cells around sporangium)

Spore inside dehisced (split open) sporangium

Abaxial (lower) surface of pinnule

Midrib of pinnule

Sorus (group of sporangia)

Midrib of pinnule

MICROGRAPH OF LOWER SURFACE OF FERTILE PINNULE

MICROGRAPH OF SPORANGIA ON LOWER SURFACE OF FERTILE PINNULE

LIFE CYCLE OF FERN

Pinna (leaflet)

Pinnule (leaflet of pinna)

Frond (leaf)

Rolled immature frond

SPOROPHYTE

Rhizome

Pinnule (leaflet of pinna)

Placenta

Indusium (flap protecting sorus)

Sorus (group of sporangia)

Sporangium (spore-producing structure)

SECTION THROUGH MATURE PINNULE

FERN
Male fern
(*Dryopteris filix-mas*)

Midrib of pinna (leaflet)

Apex of frond (leaf)

Pinna (leaflet)

Pinnule (leaflet of pinna)

Frond (leaf)

Young frond (leaf)

Rachis (main axis of pinnate leaf)

Base of old dead frond (leaf)

Young frond (leaf) rolled and covered by ramenta

Ramentum (brown scale)

Rhizome

Sporangium splits and releases spores

Annulus ruptures at weak point

Spore

RELEASE OF SPORES FROM SPORANGIUM

Spore

Filament develops into prothallus

Rhizoid

GERMINATION OF SPORE

Antheridium (male sex organ)

Archegonium (female sex organ)

Prothallus (free-living gametophyte)

Rhizoid

GAMETOPHYTE PRODUCES GAMETES

Antheridium (male sex organ)

Oosphere (female gamete)

Antherozoid (male gamete) swims to oosphere

Archegonium (female sex organ)

FERTILIZATION

Vascular bundle

Sclerenchyma (strengthening tissue)

Phloem

Xylem

Vascular tissue

Epidermis (outer layer of cells)

Parenchyma (packing tissue)

MICROGRAPH OF CROSS SECTION THROUGH FERN RACHIS

Adventitious root

Primary leaf of growing sporophyte

Remains of gametophyte

FERTILIZED OOSPHERE GROWS INTO NEW SPOROPHYTE PLANT

15

Gymnosperms 1

THE GYMNOSPERMS ARE FOUR RELATED PHYLA of seed-producing plants: Their seeds, however, lack the protective outer covering which surrounds the seeds of flowering plants. Typically, gymnosperms are woody, perennial shrubs or trees, with stems, leaves, roots, and a well-developed vascular (transport) system. The reproductive structures in most gymnosperms are cones. Male cones produce microspores in which male gametes (sex cells) develop; female cones produce megaspores in which female gametes develop. Microspores are blown by the wind to female cones, male and female gametes fuse during fertilization, and a seed develops. The four gymnosperm phyla are the conifers (phylum Coniferophyta), mostly tall trees; cycads (phylum Cycadophyta), small palm-like trees; the ginkgo or maidenhair tree (phylum Ginkgophyta), a tall tree with bilobed leaves; and gnetophytes (phylum Gnetophyta) a diverse group of plants, mainly shrubs, but also including the horizontally growing welwitschia.

LIFE CYCLE OF SCOTS PINE
(Pinus sylvestris)

Needle (foliage leaf)

Cone

Ovuliferous scale (ovule-/seed-bearing structure)

MALE CONES   **YOUNG FEMALE CONE**

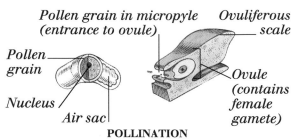

Pollen grain in micropyle (entrance to ovule)

Ovuliferous scale

Pollen grain

Nucleus

Air sac

Ovule (contains female gamete)

POLLINATION

Integument (outer part of ovule)

Archegonium (containing female gamete)

Pollen tube (carries male gamete from pollen grain to ovum)

FERTILIZATION

SCALE AND SEEDS
Pine
(Pinus sp.)

Ovuliferous scale (ovule-/seed-bearing structure)

Wing scar

Wing of seed derived from ovuliferous scale

Seed

Seed

Point of attachment to axis of cone

Seed scar

OVULIFEROUS SCALE FROM THIRD-YEAR FEMALE CONE

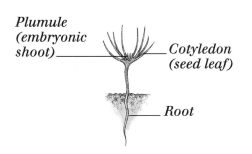

Ovuliferous scale (ovule-/seed-bearing structure)

Seed

Seed

Wing

MATURE FEMALE CONE AND WINGED SEED

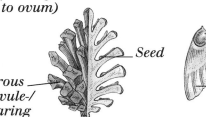

Plumule (embryonic shoot)

Cotyledon (seed leaf)

Root

GERMINATION OF PINE SEEDLING

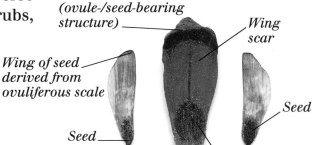

Microsporangium (structure in which pollen grains are formed)

Microsporophyll (modified leaf carrying microsporangia)

Axis of cone

Scale leaf

Ovuliferous scale (ovule-/seed-bearing structure)

MICROGRAPH OF LONGITUDINAL SECTION THROUGH YOUNG MALE CONE

Ovule (contains female gametes)

Bract scale

Axis of cone

MICROGRAPH OF LONGITUDINAL SECTION THROUGH SECOND-YEAR FEMALE CONE

WELWITSCHIA
(Welwitschia mirabilis)

Frayed end of leaf

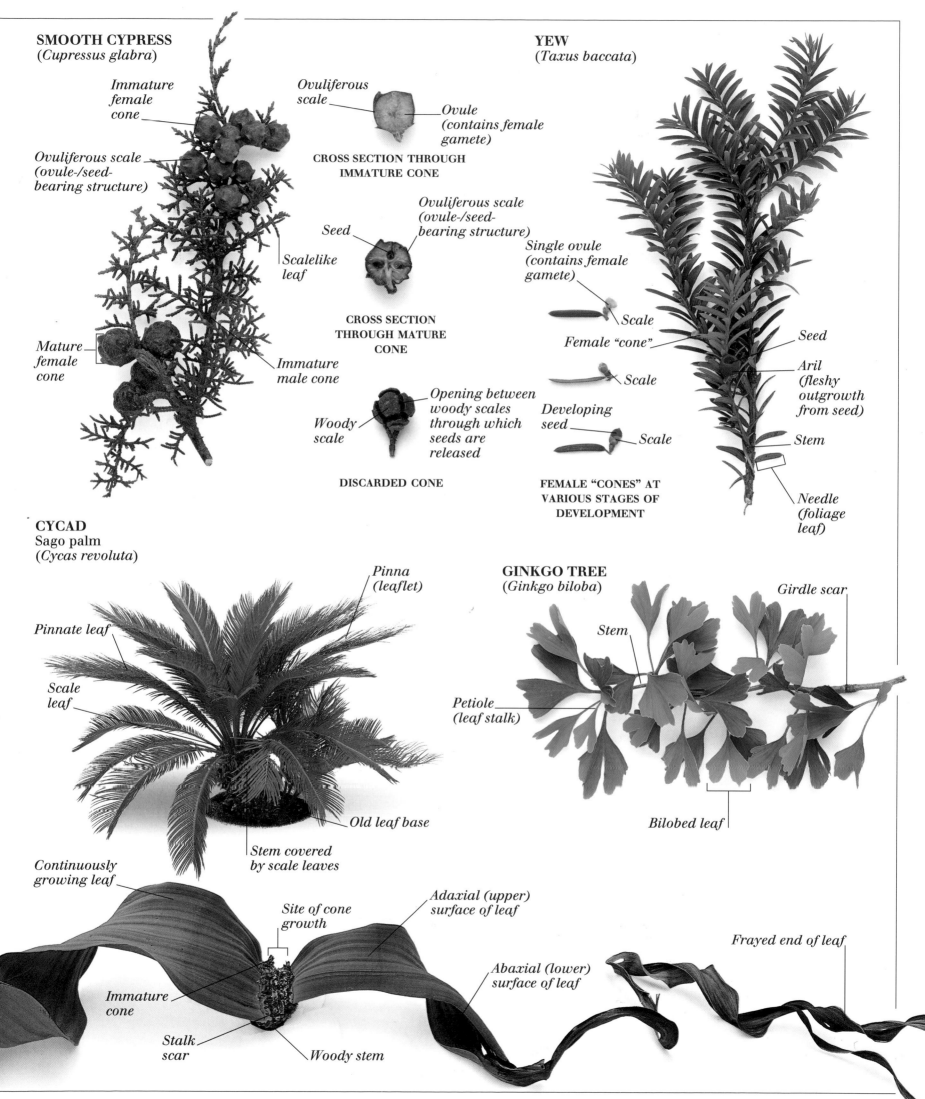

SMOOTH CYPRESS
(*Cupressus glabra*)

Immature female cone

Ovuliferous scale (ovule-/seed-bearing structure)

Mature female cone

Scalelike leaf

Immature male cone

Ovuliferous scale

Ovule (contains female gamete)

CROSS SECTION THROUGH IMMATURE CONE

Ovuliferous scale (ovule-/seed-bearing structure)

Seed

CROSS SECTION THROUGH MATURE CONE

Woody scale

Opening between woody scales through which seeds are released

DISCARDED CONE

YEW
(*Taxus baccata*)

Single ovule (contains female gamete)

Scale

Female "cone"

Scale

Developing seed

Scale

FEMALE "CONES" AT VARIOUS STAGES OF DEVELOPMENT

Seed

Aril (fleshy outgrowth from seed)

Stem

Needle (foliage leaf)

CYCAD
Sago palm
(*Cycas revoluta*)

Pinnate leaf

Scale leaf

Pinna (leaflet)

Old leaf base

Stem covered by scale leaves

Continuously growing leaf

Site of cone growth

Immature cone

Stalk scar

Woody stem

Adaxial (upper) surface of leaf

Abaxial (lower) surface of leaf

GINKGO TREE
(*Ginkgo biloba*)

Stem

Girdle scar

Petiole (leaf stalk)

Bilobed leaf

Frayed end of leaf

Gymnosperms 2

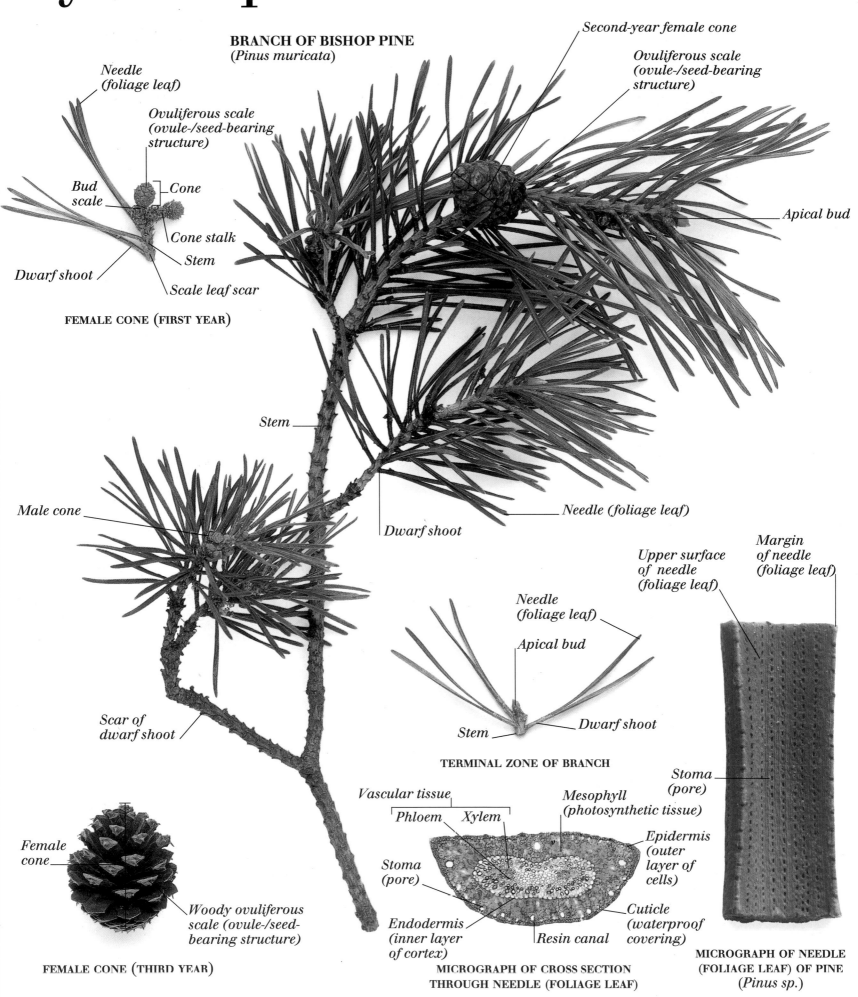

BRANCH OF BISHOP PINE
(*Pinus muricata*)

*Needle
(foliage leaf)*

*Ovuliferous scale
(ovule-/seed-bearing
structure)*

*Bud
scale*

Cone

Dwarf shoot

Cone stalk

Stem

Scale leaf scar

FEMALE CONE (FIRST YEAR)

Second-year female cone

*Ovuliferous scale
(ovule-/seed-bearing
structure)*

Apical bud

Stem

Male cone

Needle (foliage leaf)

Dwarf shoot

*Scar of
dwarf shoot*

*Female
cone*

*Woody ovuliferous
scale (ovule-/seed-
bearing structure)*

FEMALE CONE (THIRD YEAR)

*Upper surface
of needle
(foliage leaf)*

*Margin
of needle
(foliage leaf)*

*Needle
(foliage leaf)*

Apical bud

Stem

Dwarf shoot

TERMINAL ZONE OF BRANCH

*Stoma
(pore)*

Vascular tissue

Phloem   *Xylem*

*Mesophyll
(photosynthetic tissue)*

*Stoma
(pore)*

*Epidermis
(outer
layer of
cells)*

*Endodermis
(inner layer
of cortex)*

Resin canal

*Cuticle
(waterproof
covering)*

**MICROGRAPH OF CROSS SECTION
THROUGH NEEDLE (FOLIAGE LEAF)**

**MICROGRAPH OF NEEDLE
(FOLIAGE LEAF) OF PINE**
(*Pinus sp.*)

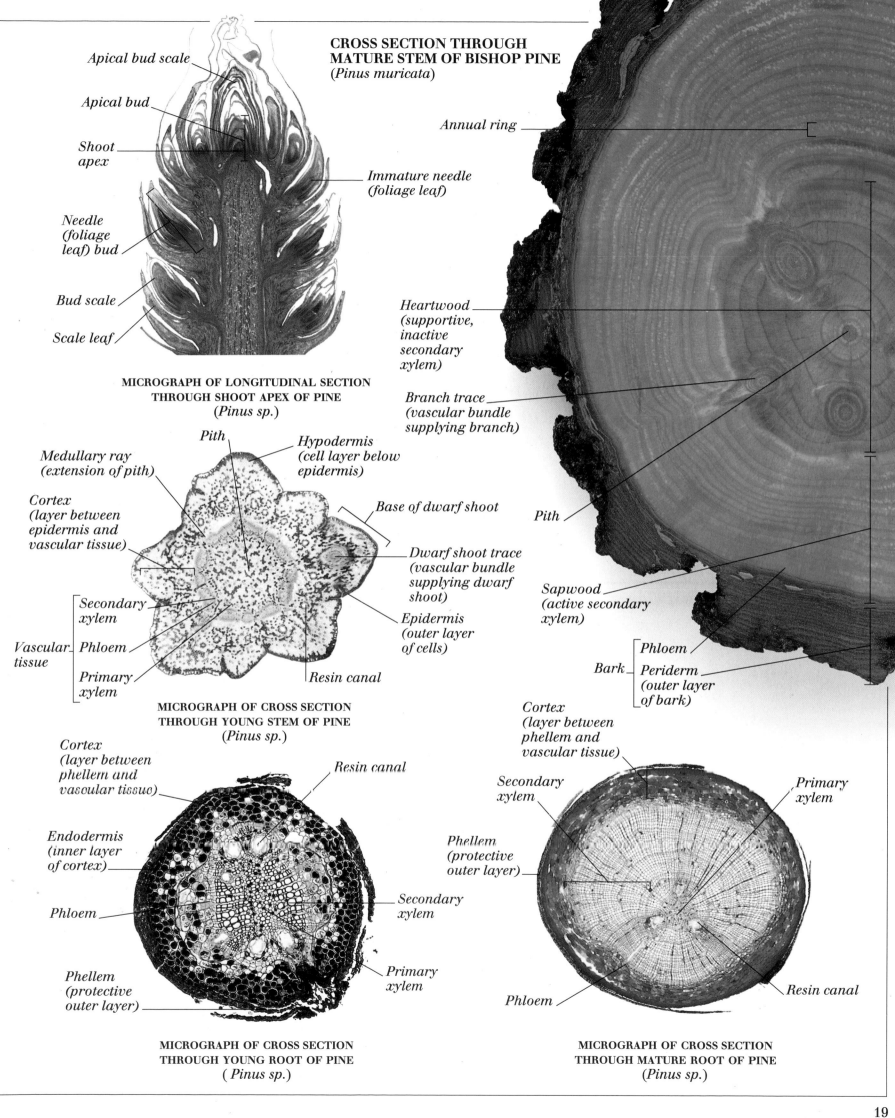

Apical bud scale

Apical bud

Shoot apex

Needle (foliage leaf) bud

Bud scale

Scale leaf

CROSS SECTION THROUGH MATURE STEM OF BISHOP PINE
(Pinus muricata)

Annual ring

Immature needle (foliage leaf)

Heartwood (supportive, inactive secondary xylem)

Branch trace (vascular bundle supplying branch)

MICROGRAPH OF LONGITUDINAL SECTION THROUGH SHOOT APEX OF PINE
(Pinus sp.)

Pith

Medullary ray (extension of pith)

Cortex (layer between epidermis and vascular tissue)

Hypodermis (cell layer below epidermis)

Base of dwarf shoot

Dwarf shoot trace (vascular bundle supplying dwarf shoot)

Epidermis (outer layer of cells)

Pith

Secondary xylem

Vascular tissue

Phloem

Primary xylem

Resin canal

Sapwood (active secondary xylem)

Bark

Phloem

Periderm (outer layer of bark)

MICROGRAPH OF CROSS SECTION THROUGH YOUNG STEM OF PINE
(Pinus sp.)

Cortex (layer between phellem and vascular tissue)

Resin canal

Endodermis (inner layer of cortex)

Phloem

Secondary xylem

Phellem (protective outer layer)

Primary xylem

Cortex (layer between phellem and vascular tissue)

Phellem (protective outer layer)

Secondary xylem

Primary xylem

Phloem

Resin canal

MICROGRAPH OF CROSS SECTION THROUGH YOUNG ROOT OF PINE
(Pinus sp.)

MICROGRAPH OF CROSS SECTION THROUGH MATURE ROOT OF PINE
(Pinus sp.)

Monocotyledons and dicotyledons

FLOWERING PLANTS (PHYLUM ANGIOSPERMOPHYTA) are divided into two classes: monocotyledons (class Monocotyledoneae) and dicotyledons (class Dicotyledoneae). Typically, monocotyledons have seeds with one cotyledon (seed leaf); their foliage leaves are narrow with parallel veins; the flower components occur in multiples of three; sepals and petals are indistinguishable and are known as tepals; vascular (transport) tissues are scattered in random bundles throughout the stem; and, because they lack stem cambium (actively dividing cells that produce wood), most monocotyledons are herbaceous (see pp. 22-23). Dicotyledons have seeds with two cotyledons; leaves are broad with a central midrib and branched veins; flower parts occur in multiples of four or five; sepals are generally small and green; petals are large and colorful; vascular bundles are arranged in a ring around the edge of the stem; and, because many dicotyledons possess wood-producing stem cambium, there are woody forms (see pp. 24-25) as well as herbaceous ones.

CROSS SECTION THROUGH MONOCOTYLEDONOUS LEAF BASES

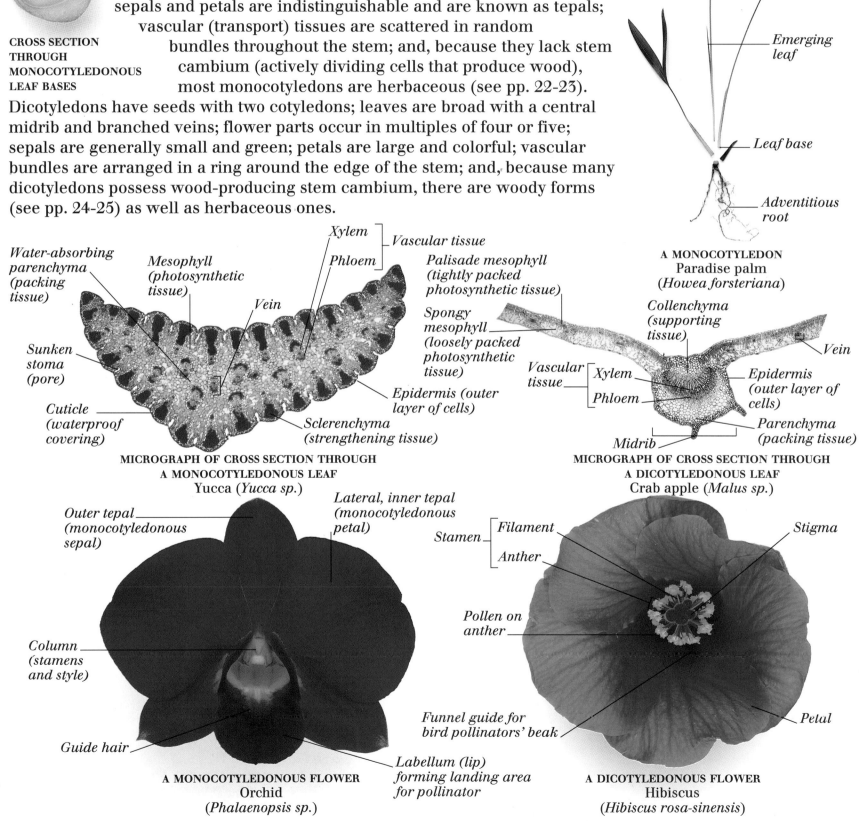

COMPARISONS BETWEEN MONOCOTYLEDONS AND DICOTYLEDONS

Vein (parallel venation)
Leaflet
Petiole (leaf stalk)
Emerging leaf
Leaf base
Adventitious root

A MONOCOTYLEDON
Paradise palm
(Howea forsteriana)

Water-absorbing parenchyma (packing tissue)
Mesophyll (photosynthetic tissue)
Xylem
Phloem
Vascular tissue
Vein
Sunken stoma (pore)
Cuticle (waterproof covering)
Epidermis (outer layer of cells)
Sclerenchyma (strengthening tissue)

MICROGRAPH OF CROSS SECTION THROUGH
A MONOCOTYLEDONOUS LEAF
Yucca (Yucca sp.)

Palisade mesophyll (tightly packed photosynthetic tissue)
Spongy mesophyll (loosely packed photosynthetic tissue)
Collenchyma (supporting tissue)
Vein
Vascular tissue
Xylem
Phloem
Epidermis (outer layer of cells)
Parenchyma (packing tissue)
Midrib

MICROGRAPH OF CROSS SECTION THROUGH
A DICOTYLEDONOUS LEAF
Crab apple (Malus sp.)

Outer tepal (monocotyledonous sepal)
Lateral, inner tepal (monocotyledonous petal)
Stamen
Filament
Anther
Stigma
Pollen on anther
Column (stamens and style)
Guide hair
Funnel guide for bird pollinators' beak
Labellum (lip) forming landing area for pollinator
Petal

A MONOCOTYLEDONOUS FLOWER
Orchid
(Phalaenopsis sp.)

A DICOTYLEDONOUS FLOWER
Hibiscus
(Hibiscus rosa-sinensis)

20

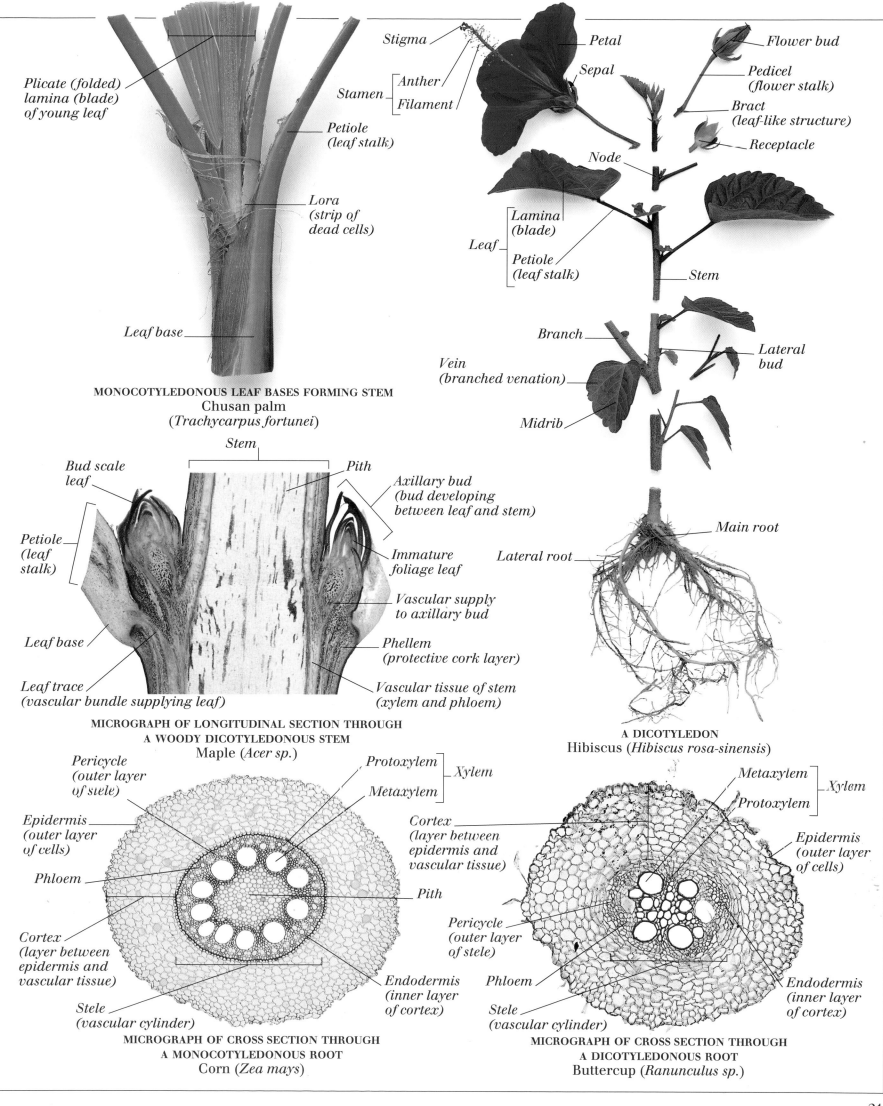

Plicate (folded) lamina (blade) of young leaf

Petiole (leaf stalk)

Lora (strip of dead cells)

Leaf base

MONOCOTYLEDONOUS LEAF BASES FORMING STEM
Chusan palm
(*Trachycarpus fortunei*)

Stigma

Petal

Sepal

Anther
Stamen
Filament

Flower bud

Pedicel (flower stalk)

Bract (leaf-like structure)

Receptacle

Node

Lamina (blade)
Leaf
Petiole (leaf stalk)

Stem

Branch

Lateral bud

Vein (branched venation)

Midrib

Bud scale leaf

Stem

Pith

Axillary bud (bud developing between leaf and stem)

Petiole (leaf stalk)

Immature foliage leaf

Vascular supply to axillary bud

Leaf base

Leaf trace (vascular bundle supplying leaf)

Phellem (protective cork layer)

Vascular tissue of stem (xylem and phloem)

MICROGRAPH OF LONGITUDINAL SECTION THROUGH A WOODY DICOTYLEDONOUS STEM
Maple (*Acer sp.*)

Main root

Lateral root

A DICOTYLEDON
Hibiscus (*Hibiscus rosa-sinensis*)

Pericycle (outer layer of stele)

Protoxylem
Xylem
Metaxylem

Metaxylem
Xylem
Protoxylem

Epidermis (outer layer of cells)

Cortex (layer between epidermis and vascular tissue)

Epidermis (outer layer of cells)

Phloem

Pith

Cortex (layer between epidermis and vascular tissue)

Pericycle (outer layer of stele)

Stele (vascular cylinder)

Endodermis (inner layer of cortex)

Phloem

Endodermis (inner layer of cortex)

Stele (vascular cylinder)

MICROGRAPH OF CROSS SECTION THROUGH A MONOCOTYLEDONOUS ROOT
Corn (*Zea mays*)

MICROGRAPH OF CROSS SECTION THROUGH A DICOTYLEDONOUS ROOT
Buttercup (*Ranunculus sp.*)

21

Herbaceous flowering plants

HERBACEOUS FLOWERING PLANTS TYPICALLY HAVE GREEN NON-WOODY STEMS, and tend to be relatively short-lived. Many herbaceous plants live for only one or two years. Annuals (such as sweet peas) grow from seed, produce flowers and then seeds, and die within a single year. Biennials (like carrots) have a two-year life cycle. In the first year, seeds grow into plants, which produce leaves and store food in underground storage organs; the stems and foliage then die in winter. In the second year, new stems grow from the storage organs, produce leaves, flowers, and seeds, and then die. Some herbaceous plants (such as potatoes) are perennial. They grow back year after year, producing shoots and flowers in spring, storing food in underground tubers or rhizomes during summer, dying in autumn, and surviving underground during winter.

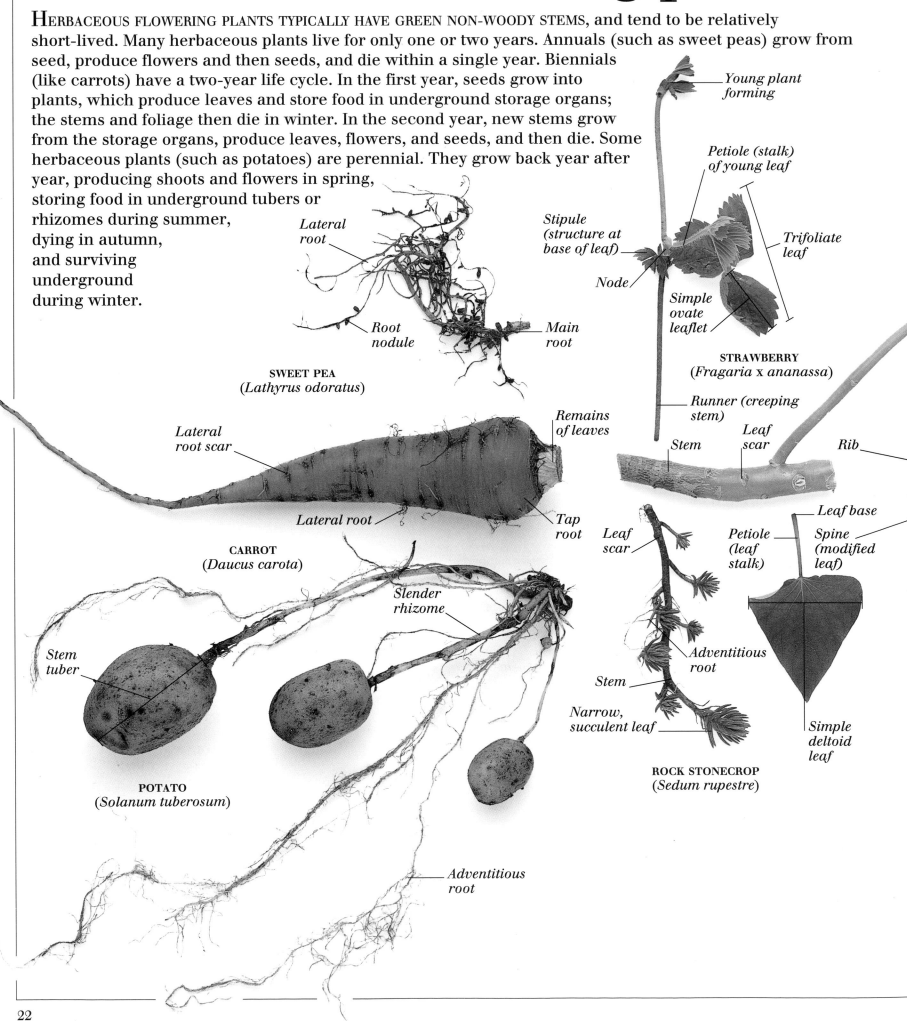

Young plant forming

Petiole (stalk) of young leaf

Stipule (structure at base of leaf)

Trifoliate leaf

Node

Simple ovate leaflet

Lateral root

Root nodule

Main root

STRAWBERRY
(*Fragaria* x *ananassa*)

SWEET PEA
(*Lathyrus odoratus*)

Runner (creeping stem)

Remains of leaves

Lateral root scar

Stem

Leaf scar

Rib

Leaf base

Lateral root

Tap root

Petiole (leaf stalk)

Spine (modified leaf)

CARROT
(*Daucus carota*)

Leaf scar

Slender rhizome

Stem tuber

Adventitious root

Stem

Simple deltoid leaf

Narrow, succulent leaf

ROCK STONECROP
(*Sedum rupestre*)

POTATO
(*Solanum tuberosum*)

Adventitious root

PARTS OF HERBACEOUS FLOWERING PLANTS

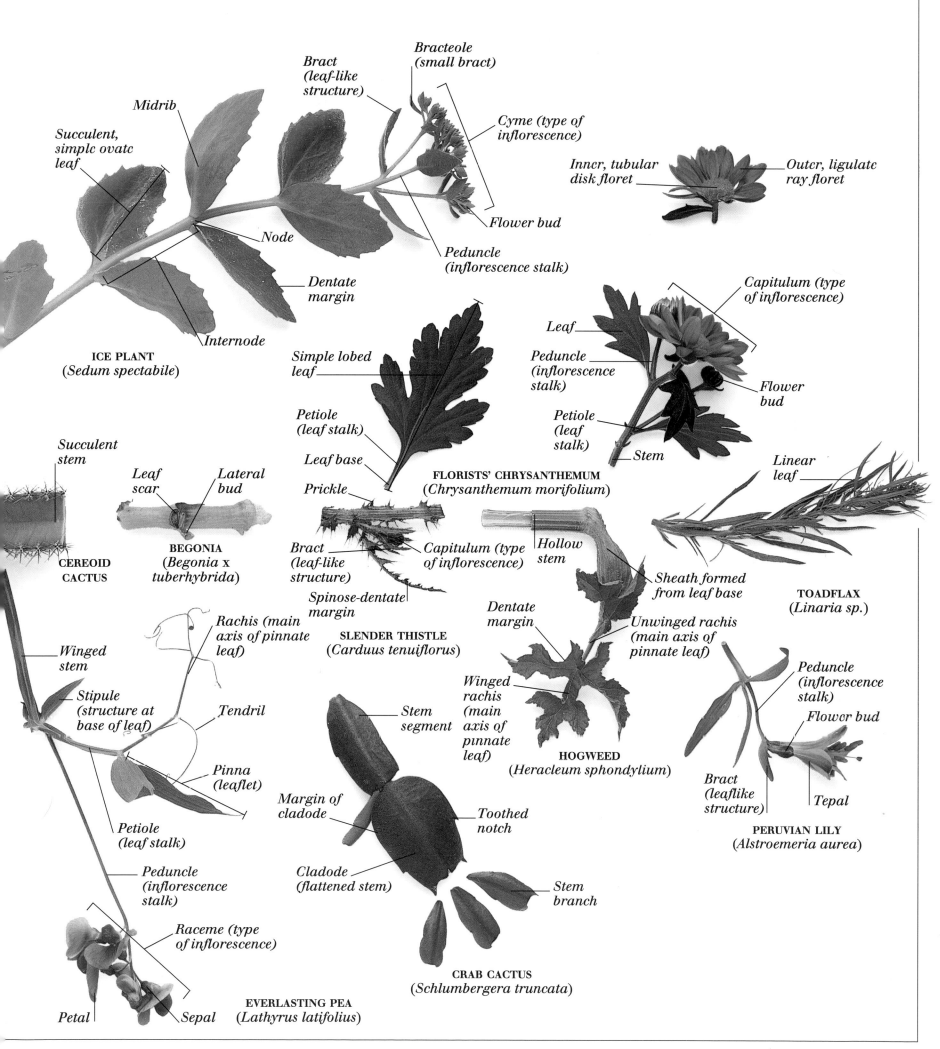

Bracteole
(small bract)

Bract
(leaf-like
structure)

Cyme (type of
inflorescence)

Midrib

Succulent,
simple ovate
leaf

Inner, tubular
disk floret

Outer, ligulate
ray floret

Flower bud

Node

Peduncle
(inflorescence stalk)

Dentate
margin

Capitulum (type
of inflorescence)

Internode

Leaf

Peduncle
(inflorescence
stalk)

ICE PLANT
(*Sedum spectabile*)

Simple lobed
leaf

Flower
bud

Petiole
(leaf stalk)

Petiole
(leaf
stalk)

Succulent
stem

Leaf base

Stem

Linear
leaf

Leaf
scar

Lateral
bud

Prickle

FLORISTS' CHRYSANTHEMUM
(*Chrysanthemum morifolium*)

**CEREOID
CACTUS**

BEGONIA
(*Begonia x
tuberhybrida*)

Hollow
stem

Bract
(leaf-like
structure)

Capitulum (type
of inflorescence)

Sheath formed
from leaf base

TOADFLAX
(*Linaria sp.*)

Rachis (main
axis of pinnate
leaf)

Spinose-dentate
margin

SLENDER THISTLE
(*Carduus tenuiflorus*)

Dentate
margin

Unwinged rachis
(main axis of
pinnate leaf)

Peduncle
(inflorescence
stalk)

Winged
stem

Tendril

Stipule
(structure at
base of leaf)

Winged
rachis
(main
axis of
pinnate
leaf)

Flower bud

Pinna
(leaflet)

Stem
segment

HOGWEED
(*Heracleum sphondylium*)

Petiole
(leaf stalk)

Margin of
cladode

Toothed
notch

Bract
(leaflike
structure)

Tepal

Peduncle
(inflorescence
stalk)

Cladode
(flattened stem)

Stem
branch

PERUVIAN LILY
(*Alstroemeria aurea*)

Raceme (type
of inflorescence)

CRAB CACTUS
(*Schlumbergera truncata*)

Petal

Sepal

EVERLASTING PEA
(*Lathyrus latifolius*)

Woody flowering plants

WOODY FLOWERING PLANTS ARE PERENNIAL: They continue to grow and reproduce for many years. They have one or more permanent stems above ground and numerous smaller branches. The stems and branches have a strong woody core that supports the plant and contains vascular tissue for transporting water and nutrients. Outside the woody core is a layer of tough, protective bark, which has lenticels (tiny pores) to allow gases to pass through. Woody flowering plants may be shrubs, which have several stems rising from the soil; bushes, which are shrubs with dense branching and foliage; or trees, which typically have a single upright stem (the trunk) that bears branches. Deciduous woody plants (like roses) shed all their leaves once a year and remain leafless during winter. Evergreen woody plants (such as ivy) shed their leaves gradually, so they retain full leaf cover throughout the year.

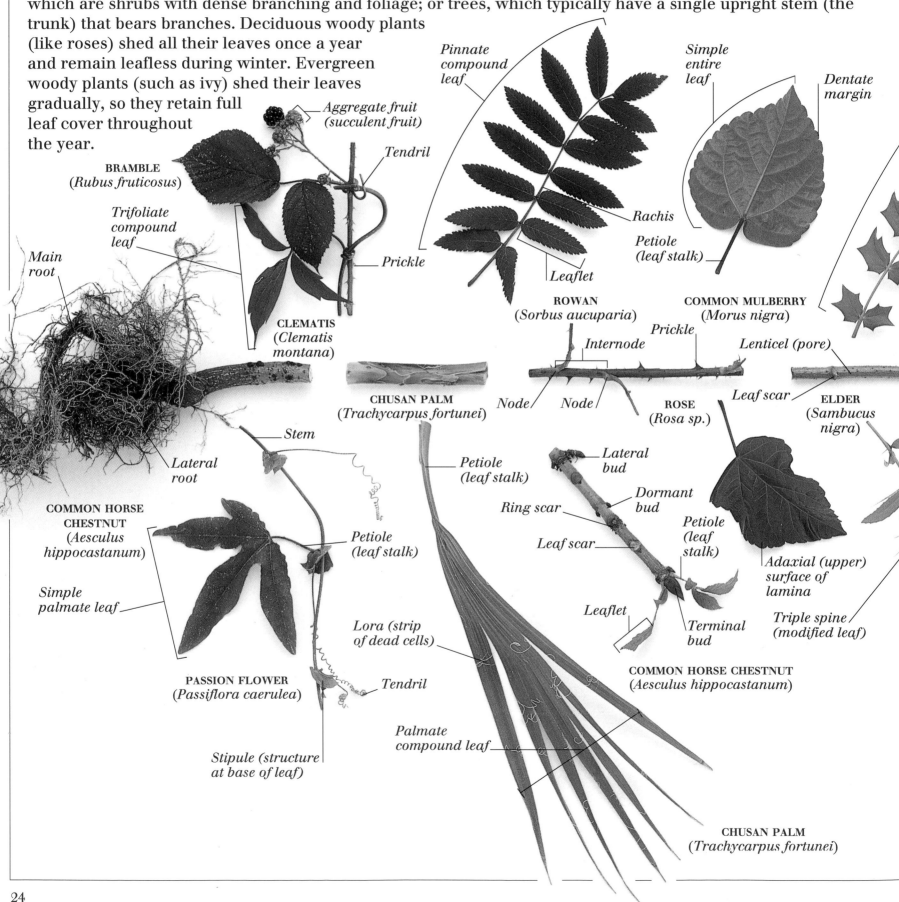

Aggregate fruit
(succulent fruit)

Tendril

BRAMBLE
(Rubus fruticosus)

Trifoliate
compound
leaf

Prickle

Main
root

CLEMATIS
*(Clematis
montana)*

Pinnate
compound
leaf

Simple
entire
leaf

Dentate
margin

Rachis

Petiole
(leaf stalk)

Leaflet

ROWAN
(Sorbus aucuparia)

COMMON MULBERRY
(Morus nigra)

Internode

Prickle

Lenticel (pore)

Node   Node

Leaf scar

ROSE
(Rosa sp.)

ELDER
*(Sambucus
nigra)*

Stem

Lateral
root

**COMMON HORSE
CHESTNUT**
*(Aesculus
hippocastanum)*

Simple
palmate leaf

CHUSAN PALM
(Trachycarpus fortunei)

Petiole
(leaf stalk)

Lateral
bud

Ring scar

Dormant
bud

Leaf scar

Petiole
(leaf
stalk)

Adaxial (upper)
surface of
lamina

Petiole
(leaf stalk)

Leaflet

Terminal
bud

Triple spine
(modified leaf)

Lora (strip
of dead cells)

Tendril

PASSION FLOWER
(Passiflora caerulea)

COMMON HORSE CHESTNUT
(Aesculus hippocastanum)

Palmate
compound leaf

Stipule (structure
at base of leaf)

CHUSAN PALM
(Trachycarpus fortunei)

PARTS OF WOODY FLOWERING PLANTS

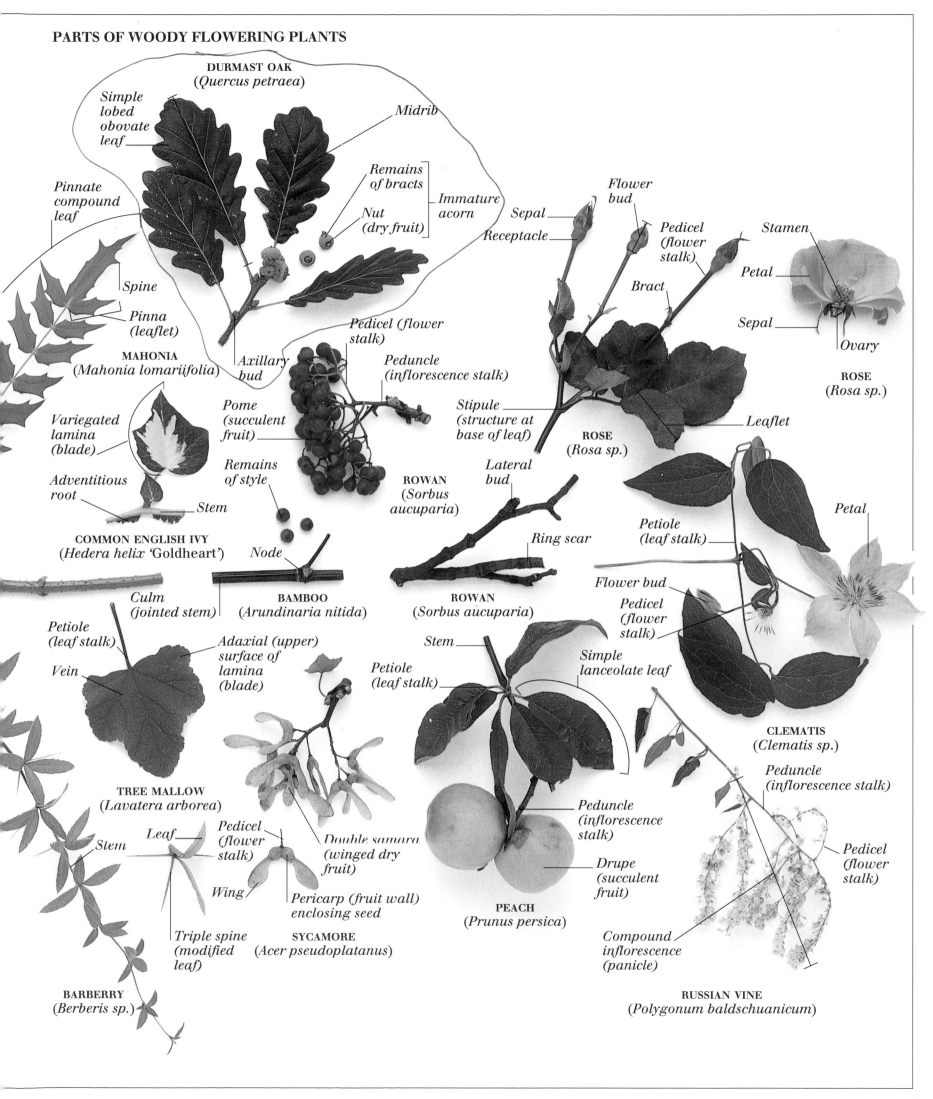

DURMAST OAK
(Quercus petraea)

Simple lobed obovate leaf

Midrib

Remains of bracts

Nut (dry fruit)

Immature acorn

Pinnate compound leaf

Spine

Pinna (leaflet)

Axillary bud

MAHONIA
(Mahonia lomariifolia)

Variegated lamina (blade)

Adventitious root

Stem

COMMON ENGLISH IVY
(Hedera helix 'Goldheart')

Pome (succulent fruit)

Remains of style

Node

Culm (jointed stem)

BAMBOO
(Arundinaria nitida)

Pedicel (flower stalk)

Peduncle (inflorescence stalk)

ROWAN
(Sorbus aucuparia)

Flower bud

Sepal

Receptacle

Pedicel (flower stalk)

Bract

Stipule (structure at base of leaf)

Leaflet

ROSE
(Rosa sp.)

Stamen

Petal

Sepal

Ovary

ROSE
(Rosa sp.)

Lateral bud

Ring scar

ROWAN
(Sorbus aucuparia)

Petiole (leaf stalk)

Flower bud

Pedicel (flower stalk)

Petal

CLEMATIS
(Clematis sp.)

Petiole (leaf stalk)

Vein

Adaxial (upper) surface of lamina (blade)

TREE MALLOW
(Lavatera arborea)

Stem

Leaf

Pedicel (flower stalk)

Wing

Triple spine (modified leaf)

Double samara (winged dry fruit)

Pericarp (fruit wall) enclosing seed

SYCAMORE
(Acer pseudoplatanus)

Stem

Petiole (leaf stalk)

Simple lanceolate leaf

Peduncle (inflorescence stalk)

Drupe (succulent fruit)

PEACH
(Prunus persica)

Peduncle (inflorescence stalk)

Pedicel (flower stalk)

Compound inflorescence (panicle)

RUSSIAN VINE
(Polygonum baldschuanicum)

BARBERRY
(Berberis sp.)

Roots

ROOTS ARE THE UNDERGROUND PARTS OF PLANTS. They have three main functions. First, they anchor the plant in the soil. Second, they absorb water and minerals from the spaces between soil particles. The roots' absorptive properties are increased by root hairs, which grow behind the root tip, allowing maximum absorption of vital substances. Third, the root is part of the plant's transport system. Xylem carries water and minerals from the roots to the stem and leaves, and phloem carries nutrients from the leaves to all parts of the root system. In addition, some roots (like carrots) are food stores. Roots have an outer epidermis covering a cortex of parenchyma (packing tissue), and a central cylinder of vascular tissue. This arrangement helps the roots resist the forces of compression as they grow through the soil.

MICROGRAPH OF PRIMARY ROOT DEVELOPMENT
Cabbage (*Brassica sp.*)

Split in testa
as seed
germinates

Cotyledon
(seed leaf)

Primary root

Testa
(seed coat)

Root hair

Root tip
(region of
cell division)

CARROT
(*Daucus carota*)

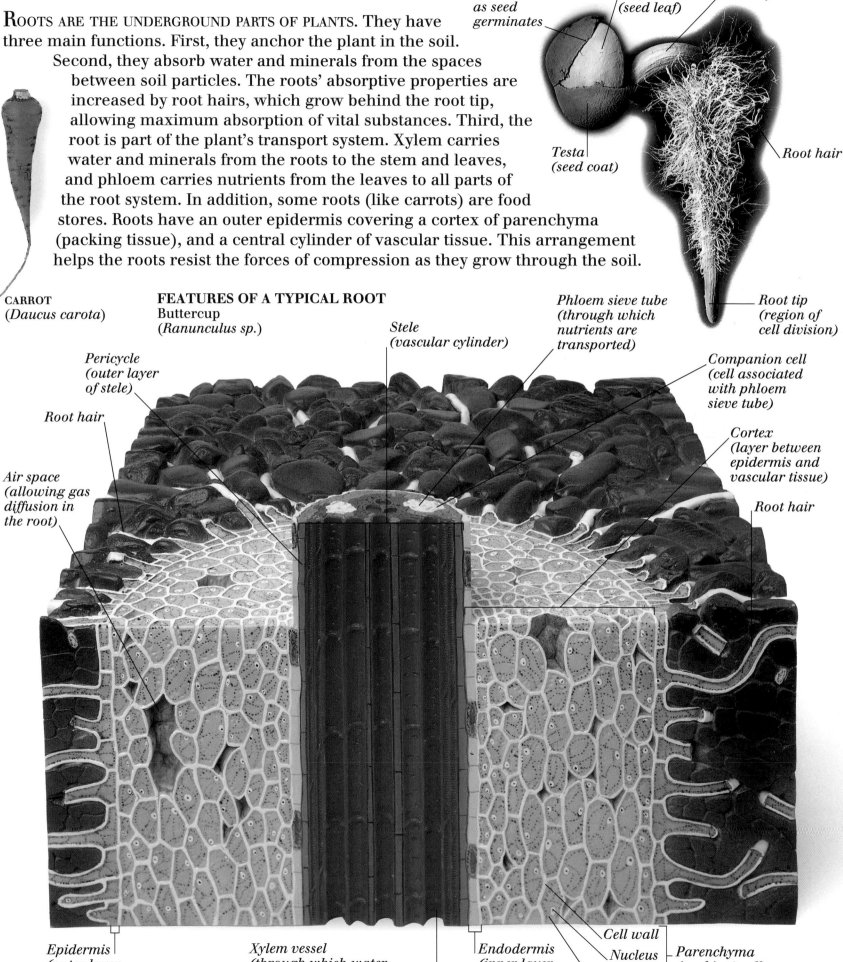

FEATURES OF A TYPICAL ROOT
Buttercup
(*Ranunculus sp.*)

Stele
(vascular cylinder)

Phloem sieve tube
(through which
nutrients are
transported)

Companion cell
(cell associated
with phloem
sieve tube)

Pericycle
(outer layer
of stele)

Root hair

Cortex
(layer between
epidermis and
vascular tissue)

Root hair

Air space
(allowing gas
diffusion in
the root)

Epidermis
(outer layer
of cells)

Xylem vessel
(through which water
and minerals are transported

Endodermis
(inner layer
of cortex)

Cell wall

Nucleus

Cytoplasm

Parenchyma
(packing) cell

26

PRIMARY ROOT AND MICROGRAPHS OF SECTIONS THROUGH ROOTS

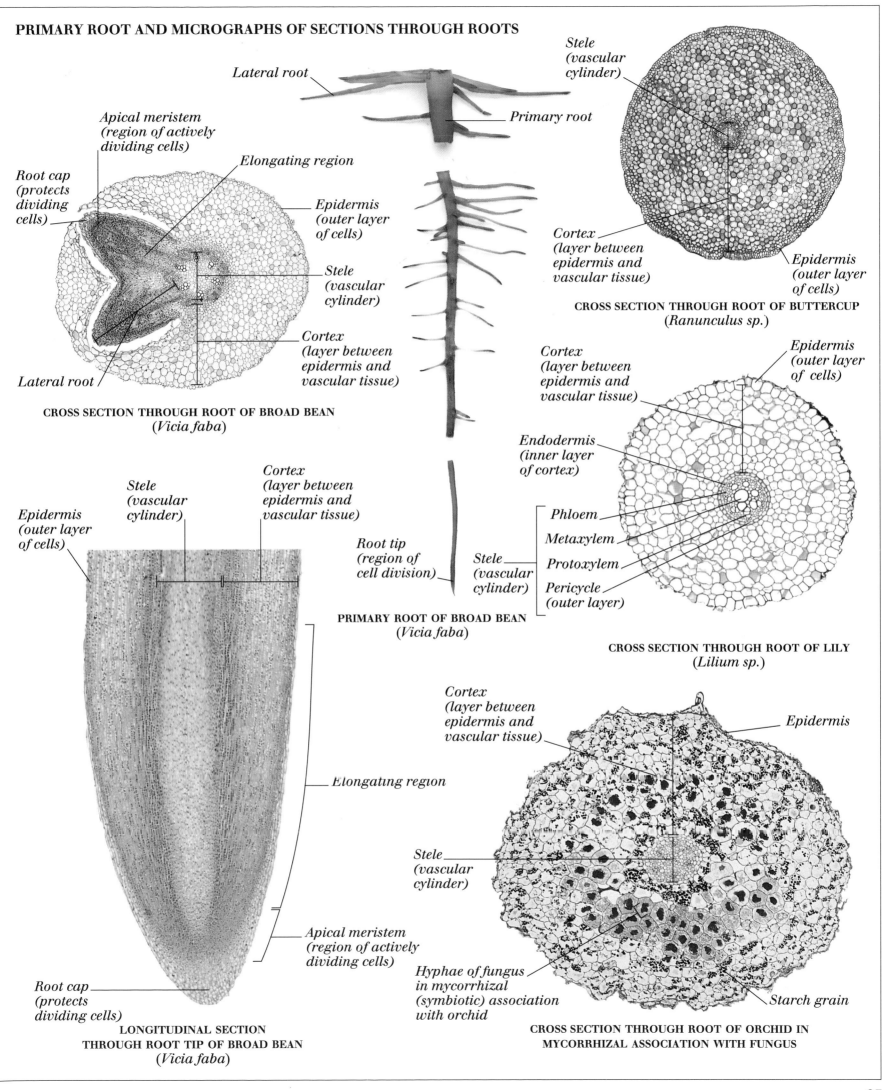

Lateral root

Primary root

Apical meristem
(region of actively
dividing cells)

Elongating region

Root cap
(protects
dividing
cells)

Epidermis
(outer layer
of cells)

Stele
(vascular
cylinder)

Cortex
(layer between
epidermis and
vascular tissue)

Lateral root

CROSS SECTION THROUGH ROOT OF BROAD BEAN
(*Vicia faba*)

Stele
(vascular
cylinder)

Cortex
(layer between
epidermis and
vascular tissue)

Epidermis
(outer layer
of cells)

Root tip
(region of
cell division)

Stele
(vascular
cylinder)

PRIMARY ROOT OF BROAD BEAN
(*Vicia faba*)

Elongating region

Apical meristem
(region of actively
dividing cells)

Root cap
(protects
dividing cells)

**LONGITUDINAL SECTION
THROUGH ROOT TIP OF BROAD BEAN**
(*Vicia faba*)

Stele
(vascular
cylinder)

Cortex
(layer between
epidermis and
vascular tissue)

Epidermis
(outer layer
of cells)

CROSS SECTION THROUGH ROOT OF BUTTERCUP
(*Ranunculus sp.*)

Cortex
(layer between
epidermis and
vascular tissue)

Epidermis
(outer layer
of cells)

Endodermis
(inner layer
of cortex)

Phloem

Metaxylem

Protoxylem

Pericycle
(outer layer)

CROSS SECTION THROUGH ROOT OF LILY
(*Lilium sp.*)

Cortex
(layer between
epidermis and
vascular tissue)

Epidermis

Stele
(vascular
cylinder)

Hyphae of fungus
in mycorrhizal
(symbiotic) association
with orchid

Starch grain

**CROSS SECTION THROUGH ROOT OF ORCHID IN
MYCORRHIZAL ASSOCIATION WITH FUNGUS**

27

Stems

THE STEM IS THE MAIN SUPPORTIVE PART OF A PLANT that grows above ground. Stems bear leaves (organs of photosynthesis), which grow at nodes; buds (shoots covered by protective scales), which grow at the stem tip (apical or terminal buds) and in the angle between a leaf and the stem (axillary or lateral buds); and flowers (reproductive structures). The stem forms part of the plant's transport system. Xylem tissue in the stem transports water and minerals from the roots to the aerial parts of the plant, and phloem tissue transports nutrients manufactured in the leaves to other parts of the plant. Stem tissues are also used for storing water and food. Herbaceous (nonwoody) stems have an outer protective epidermis covering a cortex that consists mainly of parenchyma (packing tissue) but also has some collenchyma (supporting tissue). The vascular tissue of such stems is arranged in bundles, each of which consists of xylem, phloem, and sclerenchyma (strengthening tissue). Woody stems have an outer protective layer of tough bark, which is perforated with lenticels (pores) to allow gas exchange. Inside the bark is a ring of secondary phloem, which surrounds an inner core of secondary xylem.

MICROGRAPH OF LONGITUDINAL SECTION THROUGH APEX OF STEM
Coleus sp.

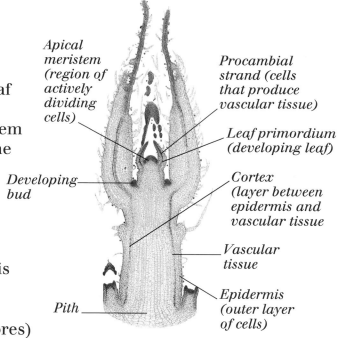

Apical meristem (region of actively dividing cells)

Procambial strand (cells that produce vascular tissue)

Leaf primordium (developing leaf)

Developing bud

Cortex (layer between epidermis and vascular tissue)

Vascular tissue

Epidermis (outer layer of cells)

Pith

YOUNG WOODY STEM
Lime
(*Tilia sp.*)

EMERGENT BUDS
London plane
(*Platanus x acerifolia*)

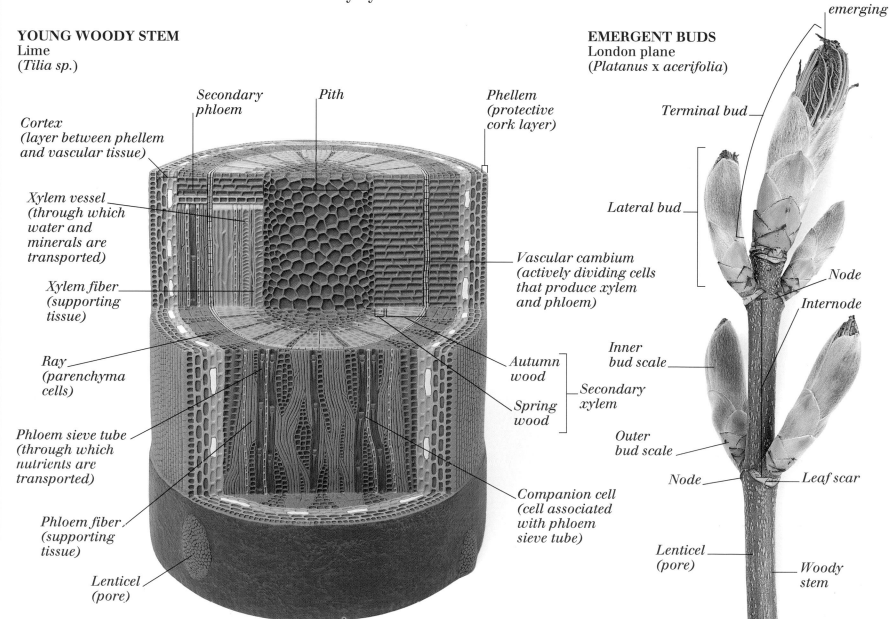

Secondary phloem

Pith

Phellem (protective cork layer)

Cortex (layer between phellem and vascular tissue)

Xylem vessel (through which water and minerals are transported)

Xylem fiber (supporting tissue)

Ray (parenchyma cells)

Phloem sieve tube (through which nutrients are transported)

Phloem fiber (supporting tissue)

Lenticel (pore)

Vascular cambium (actively dividing cells that produce xylem and phloem)

Autumn wood

Secondary xylem

Spring wood

Companion cell (cell associated with phloem sieve tube)

Young leaves emerging

Terminal bud

Lateral bud

Node

Internode

Inner bud scale

Outer bud scale

Node

Leaf scar

Lenticel (pore)

Woody stem

MICROGRAPHS OF CROSS SECTIONS THROUGH VARIOUS STEMS

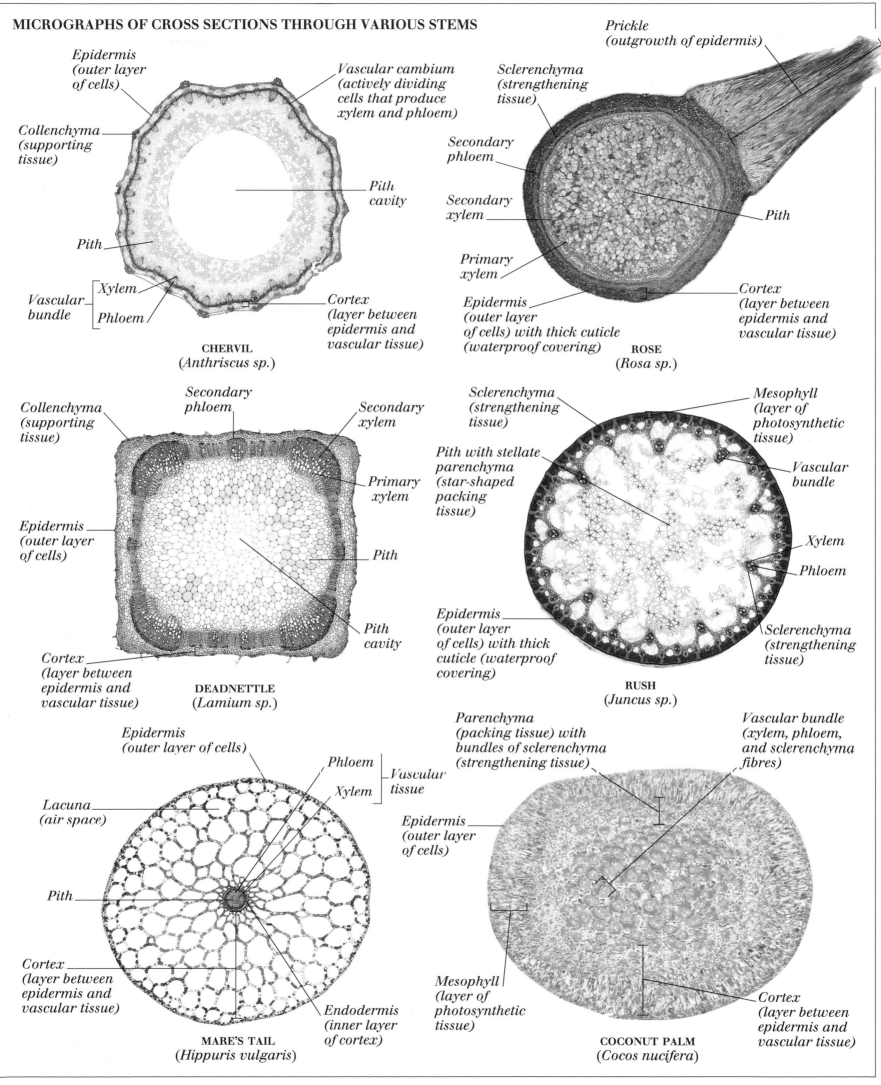

Epidermis (outer layer of cells)

Collenchyma (supporting tissue)

Pith

Vascular bundle

Xylem

Phloem

Vascular cambium (actively dividing cells that produce xylem and phloem)

Pith cavity

Cortex (layer between epidermis and vascular tissue)

CHERVIL *(Anthriscus sp.)*

Prickle (outgrowth of epidermis)

Sclerenchyma (strengthening tissue)

Secondary phloem

Secondary xylem

Primary xylem

Epidermis (outer layer of cells) with thick cuticle (waterproof covering)

Pith

Cortex (layer between epidermis and vascular tissue)

ROSE *(Rosa sp.)*

Collenchyma (supporting tissue)

Secondary phloem

Secondary xylem

Primary xylem

Epidermis (outer layer of cells)

Pith

Pith cavity

Cortex (layer between epidermis and vascular tissue)

DEADNETTLE *(Lamium sp.)*

Sclerenchyma (strengthening tissue)

Mesophyll (layer of photosynthetic tissue)

Pith with stellate parenchyma (star-shaped packing tissue)

Vascular bundle

Xylem

Phloem

Epidermis (outer layer of cells) with thick cuticle (waterproof covering)

Sclerenchyma (strengthening tissue)

RUSH *(Juncus sp.)*

Epidermis (outer layer of cells)

Phloem

Xylem

Vascular tissue

Lacuna (air space)

Pith

Cortex (layer between epidermis and vascular tissue)

Endodermis (inner layer of cortex)

MARE'S TAIL *(Hippuris vulgaris)*

Parenchyma (packing tissue) with bundles of sclerenchyma (strengthening tissue)

Vascular bundle (xylem, phloem, and sclerenchyma fibres)

Epidermis (outer layer of cells)

Mesophyll (layer of photosynthetic tissue)

Cortex (layer between epidermis and vascular tissue)

COCONUT PALM *(Cocos nucifera)*

Leaves

LEAVES ARE THE MAIN SITES OF PHOTOSYNTHESIS (see pp. 32-33) and transpiration (water loss by evaporation) in plants. A typical leaf consists of a thin, flat lamina (blade) supported by a network of veins; a petiole (leaf stalk); and a leaf base, where the petiole joins the stem. Leaves can be classified as simple, in which the lamina is a single unit, or compound, in which the lamina is divided into separate leaflets. Compound leaves may be pinnate, with pinnae (leaflets) on both sides of a rachis (main axis), or palmate, with leaflets arising from a single point at the tip of the petiole. Leaves can be classified further by the overall shape of the lamina, and by the shape of the lamina's apex, margin, and base.

CHECKERBLOOM
(*Sidalcea malviflora*)

SIMPLE LEAF SHAPES

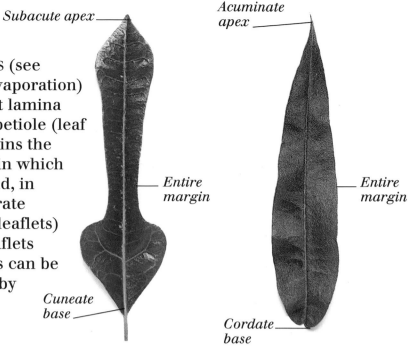

Subacute apex

Acuminate apex

Entire margin

Entire margin

Cuneate base

Cordate base

PANDURIFORM
Croton
(*Codiaeum variegatum*)

LANCEOLATE
Sea buckthorn
(*Hippophae rhamnoides*)

GENERAL LEAF FEATURES

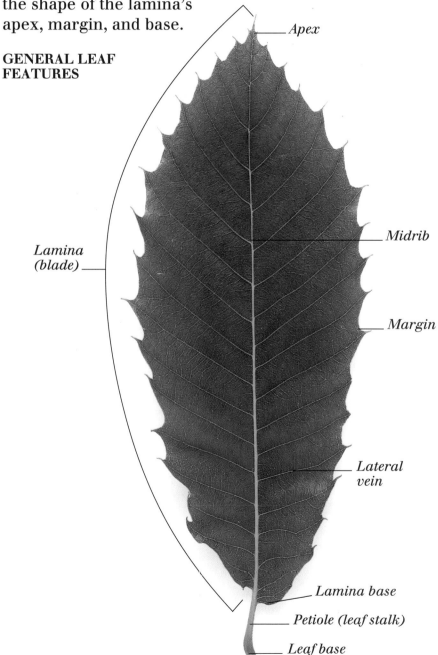

Apex

Midrib

Lamina (blade)

Margin

Lateral vein

Lamina base

Petiole (leaf stalk)

Leaf base

Spanish chestnut
(*Castanea sativa*)

COMPOUND LEAF SHAPES

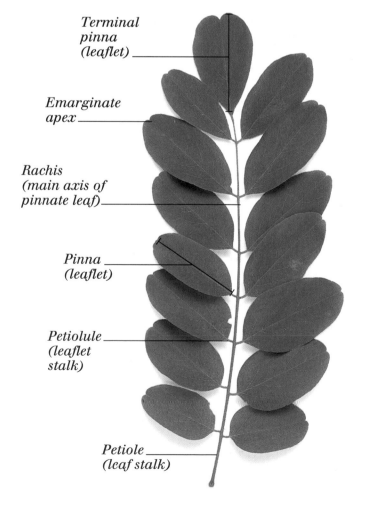

Terminal pinna (leaflet)

Emarginate apex

Rachis (main axis of pinnate leaf)

Pinna (leaflet)

Petiolule (leaflet stalk)

Petiole (leaf stalk)

ODD PINNATE
False acacia
(*Robinia pseudoacacia*)

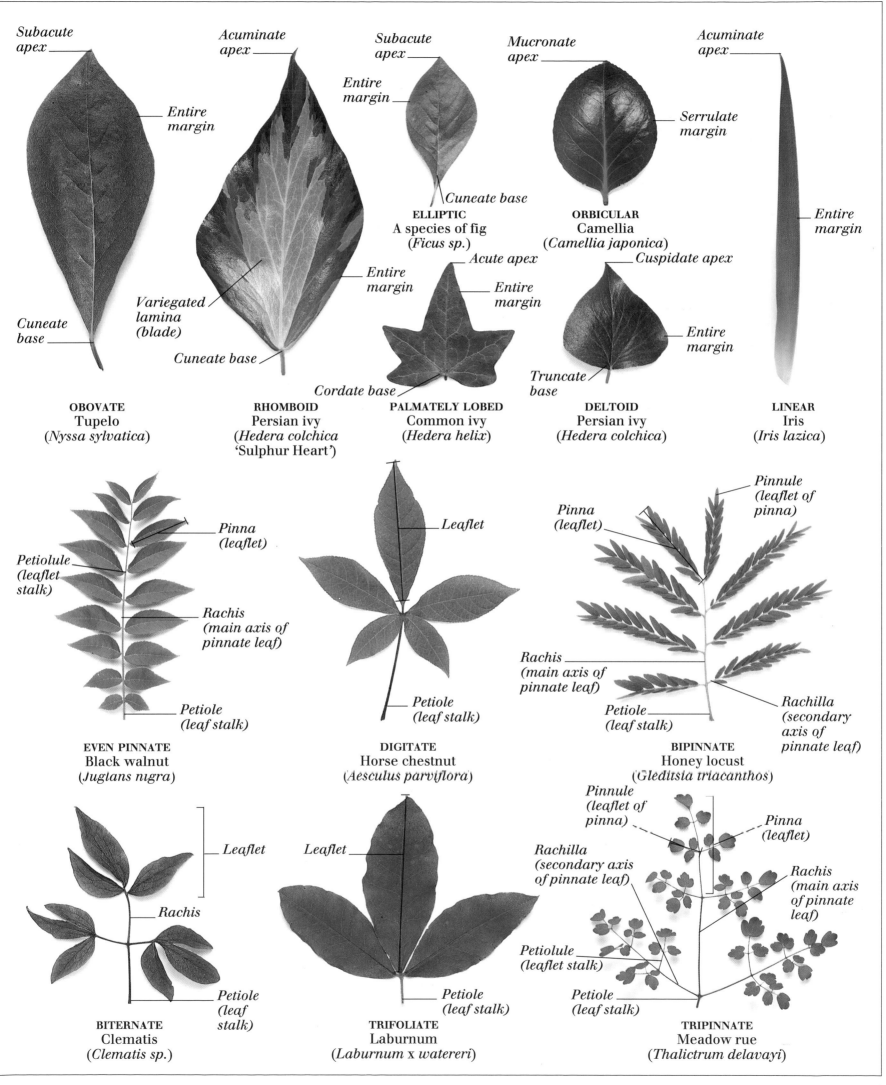

Subacute apex

Acuminate apex

Subacute apex

Mucronate apex

Acuminate apex

Entire margin

Entire margin

Serrulate margin

Cuneate base

Entire margin

Variegated lamina (blade)

Cuneate base

ELLIPTIC
A species of fig
(*Ficus sp.*)

ORBICULAR
Camellia
(*Camellia japonica*)

Entire margin

Cuneate base

Acute apex

Cuspidate apex

Entire margin

Entire margin

Entire margin

Truncate base

Cordate base

OBOVATE
Tupelo
(*Nyssa sylvatica*)

RHOMBOID
Persian ivy
(*Hedera colchica*
'Sulphur Heart')

PALMATELY LOBED
Common ivy
(*Hedera helix*)

DELTOID
Persian ivy
(*Hedera colchica*)

LINEAR
Iris
(*Iris lazica*)

Pinnule (leaflet of pinna)

Pinna (leaflet)

Leaflet

Pinna (leaflet)

Petiolule (leaflet stalk)

Rachis (main axis of pinnate leaf)

Rachis (main axis of pinnate leaf)

Rachilla (secondary axis of pinnate leaf)

Petiole (leaf stalk)

Petiole (leaf stalk)

Petiole (leaf stalk)

EVEN PINNATE
Black walnut
(*Juglans nigra*)

DIGITATE
Horse chestnut
(*Aesculus parviflora*)

BIPINNATE
Honey locust
(*Gleditsia triacanthos*)

Pinnule (leaflet of pinna)

Leaflet

Leaflet

Pinna (leaflet)

Rachis

Rachilla (secondary axis of pinnate leaf)

Rachis (main axis of pinnate leaf)

Petiole (leaf stalk)

Petiolule (leaflet stalk)

Petiole (leaf stalk)

Petiole (leaf stalk)

BITERNATE
Clematis
(*Clematis sp.*)

TRIFOLIATE
Laburnum
(*Laburnum x watereri*)

TRIPINNATE
Meadow rue
(*Thalictrum delavayi*)

Photosynthesis

PHOTOSYNTHESIS IS THE PROCESS by which plants make their food using sunlight, water, and carbon dioxide. It takes place inside special structures in leaf cells called chloroplasts. The chloroplasts contain chlorophyll, a green pigment that absorbs energy from sunlight. During photosynthesis, the absorbed energy is used to join together carbon dioxide and water to form the sugar glucose, which is the energy source for the whole plant. Oxygen, a waste product, is released into the air. Leaves are the main sites of photosynthesis and have various adaptations for that purpose. Flat laminae (blades) provide a large surface for absorbing sunlight; stomata (pores) in the lower surface of the laminae allow gases (carbon dioxide and oxygen) to pass into and out of the leaves; and an extensive network of veins brings water into the leaves and transports the glucose produced by photosynthesis to the rest of the plant.

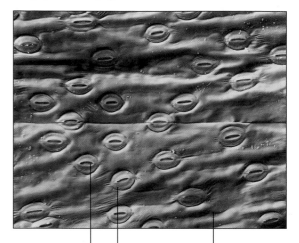

MICROGRAPH OF LEAF
Lily (*Lilium sp.*)

Stoma (pore)

Guard cell (controls opening and closing of stoma)

Lower surface of lamina (blade)

THE PROCESS OF PHOTOSYNTHESIS

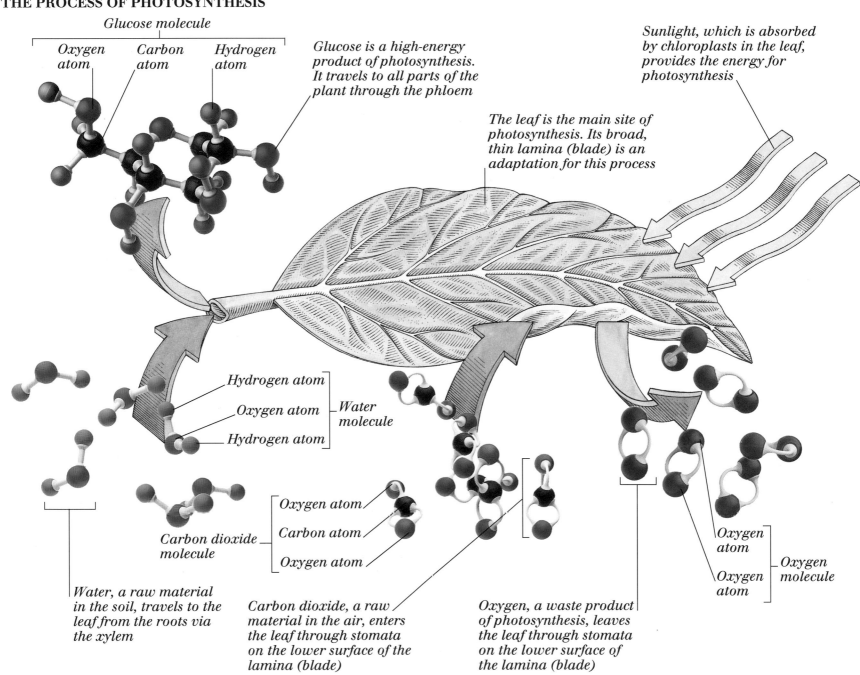

Glucose molecule

Oxygen atom

Carbon atom

Hydrogen atom

Glucose is a high-energy product of photosynthesis. It travels to all parts of the plant through the phloem

Sunlight, which is absorbed by chloroplasts in the leaf, provides the energy for photosynthesis

The leaf is the main site of photosynthesis. Its broad, thin lamina (blade) is an adaptation for this process

Hydrogen atom

Oxygen atom

Hydrogen atom

Water molecule

Carbon dioxide molecule

Oxygen atom

Carbon atom

Oxygen atom

Oxygen atom

Oxygen atom

Oxygen molecule

Water, a raw material in the soil, travels to the leaf from the roots via the xylem

Carbon dioxide, a raw material in the air, enters the leaf through stomata on the lower surface of the lamina (blade)

Oxygen, a waste product of photosynthesis, leaves the leaf through stomata on the lower surface of the lamina (blade)

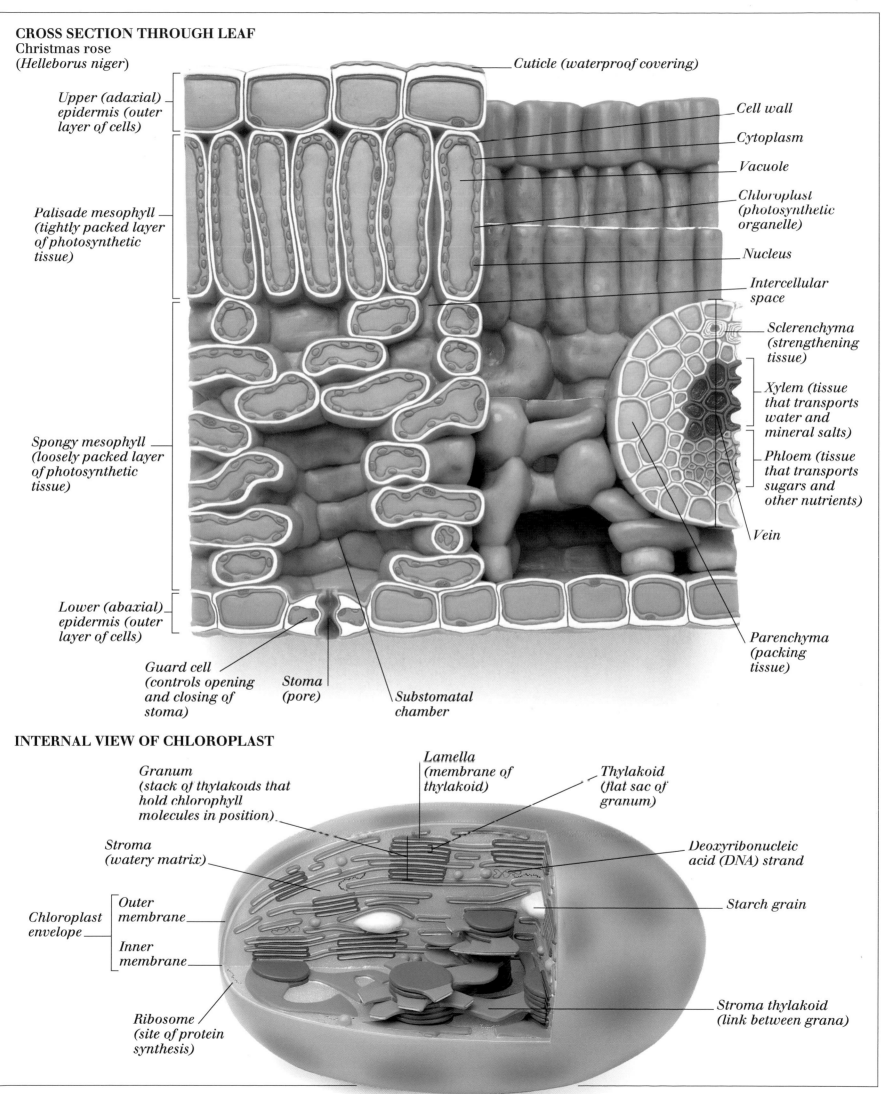

CROSS SECTION THROUGH LEAF
Christmas rose
(*Helleborus niger*)

Cuticle (waterproof covering)

Upper (adaxial) epidermis (outer layer of cells)

Cell wall

Cytoplasm

Vacuole

Chloroplast (photosynthetic organelle)

Palisade mesophyll (tightly packed layer of photosynthetic tissue)

Nucleus

Intercellular space

Sclerenchyma (strengthening tissue)

Xylem (tissue that transports water and mineral salts)

Spongy mesophyll (loosely packed layer of photosynthetic tissue)

Phloem (tissue that transports sugars and other nutrients)

Vein

Lower (abaxial) epidermis (outer layer of cells)

Guard cell (controls opening and closing of stoma)

Stoma (pore)

Substomatal chamber

Parenchyma (packing tissue)

INTERNAL VIEW OF CHLOROPLAST

Granum (stack of thylakoids that hold chlorophyll molecules in position)

Lamella (membrane of thylakoid)

Thylakoid (flat sac of granum)

Stroma (watery matrix)

Deoxyribonucleic acid (DNA) strand

Chloroplast envelope

Outer membrane

Inner membrane

Starch grain

Ribosome (site of protein synthesis)

Stroma thylakoid (link between grana)

Flowers 1

FLOWERS ARE THE SITES OF SEXUAL REPRODUCTION in flowering plants. Their component parts are arranged in whorls around the receptacle (tip of the flower stalk). The sepals (collectively called the calyx) are outermost; typically small and green, they protect the developing flower. The petals (collectively called the corolla) are typically large and brightly colored; they are found inside the sepals. In monocotyledonous flowers (see pp. 20-21), sepals and petals are indistinguishable; individually they are called tepals (collectively called the perianth). The petals surround the male and female reproductive structures (androecium and gynoecium). The androecium consists of stamens (male organs); each stamen is made up of a filament (stalk) and anther. The gynoecium has one or more carpels (female organs); each carpel consists of an ovary, style, and stigma. Some flowers (like the lily) occur singly on a pedicel (flower stalk); others (such as elder, sunflower) are arranged in a group (inflorescence) on a peduncle (inflorescence stalk).

A MONOCOTYLEDONOUS FLOWER
Lily
(*Lilium sp.*)

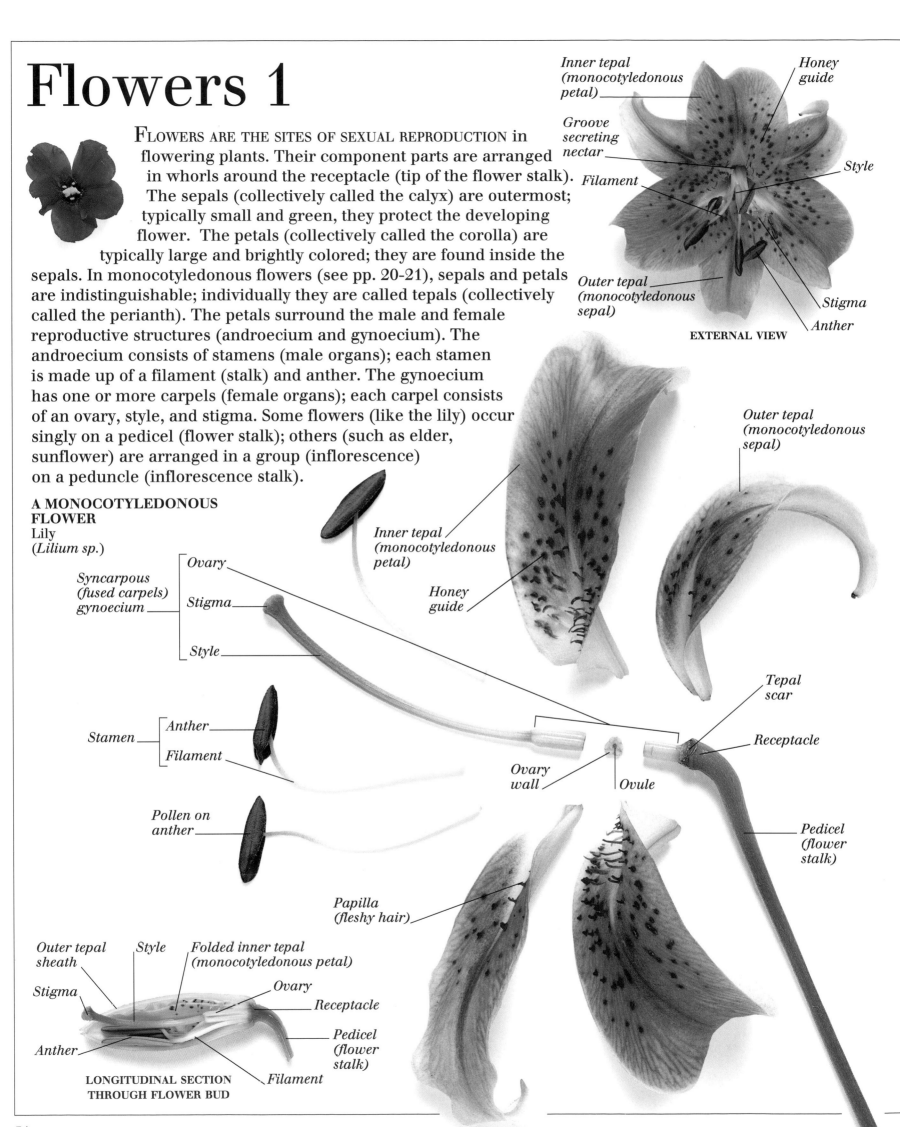

EXTERNAL VIEW

LONGITUDINAL SECTION THROUGH FLOWER BUD

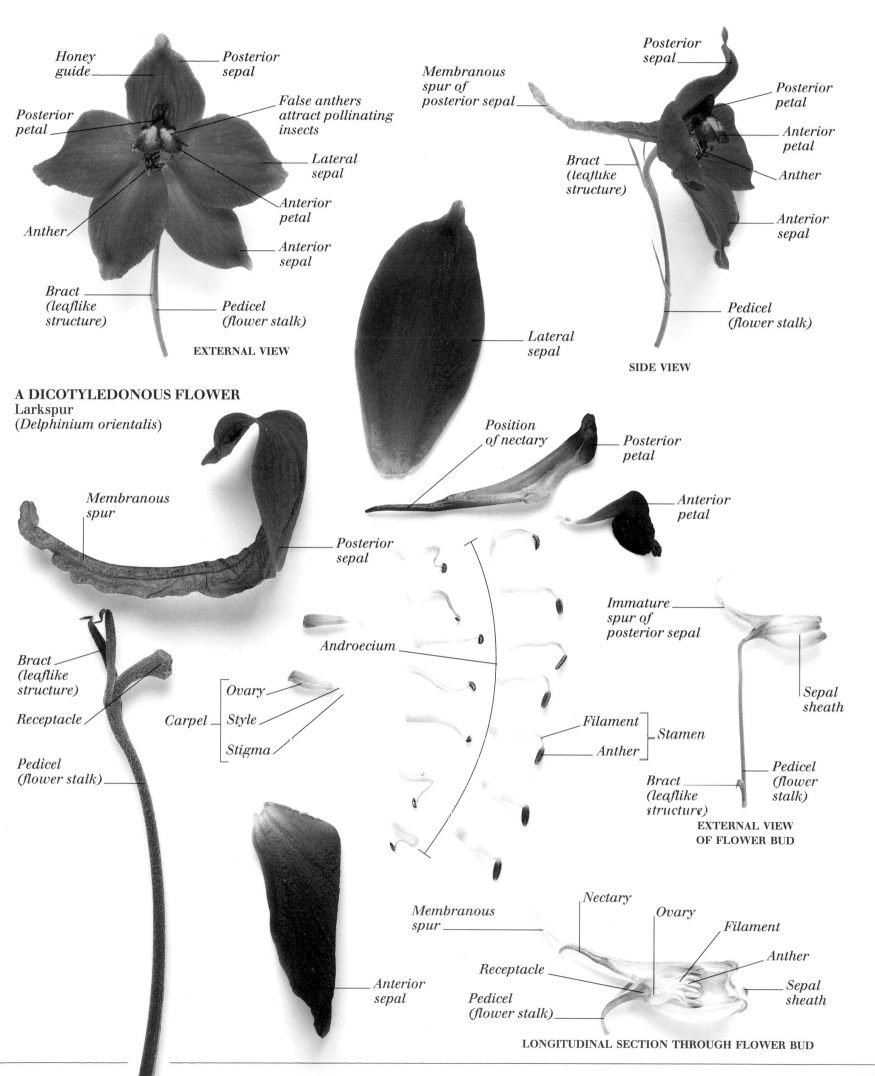

Honey
guide

Posterior
sepal

Posterior
petal

False anthers
attract pollinating
insects

Lateral
sepal

Anterior
petal

Anther

Anterior
sepal

Bract
(leaflike
structure)

Pedicel
(flower stalk)

EXTERNAL VIEW

Posterior
sepal

Membranous
spur of
posterior sepal

Posterior
petal

Anterior
petal

Anther

Bract
(leaflike
structure)

Anterior
sepal

Pedicel
(flower stalk)

Lateral
sepal

SIDE VIEW

A DICOTYLEDONOUS FLOWER
Larkspur
(*Delphinium orientalis*)

Membranous
spur

Posterior
sepal

Position
of nectary

Posterior
petal

Anterior
petal

Bract
(leaflike
structure)

Receptacle

Pedicel
(flower stalk)

Carpel

Ovary

Style

Stigma

Androecium

Filament

Anther

Stamen

Immature
spur of
posterior sepal

Sepal
sheath

Bract
(leaflike
structure)

Pedicel
(flower
stalk)

**EXTERNAL VIEW
OF FLOWER BUD**

Anterior
sepal

Membranous
spur

Pedicel
(flower stalk)

Receptacle

Nectary

Ovary

Filament

Anther

Sepal
sheath

LONGITUDINAL SECTION THROUGH FLOWER BUD

Flowers 2

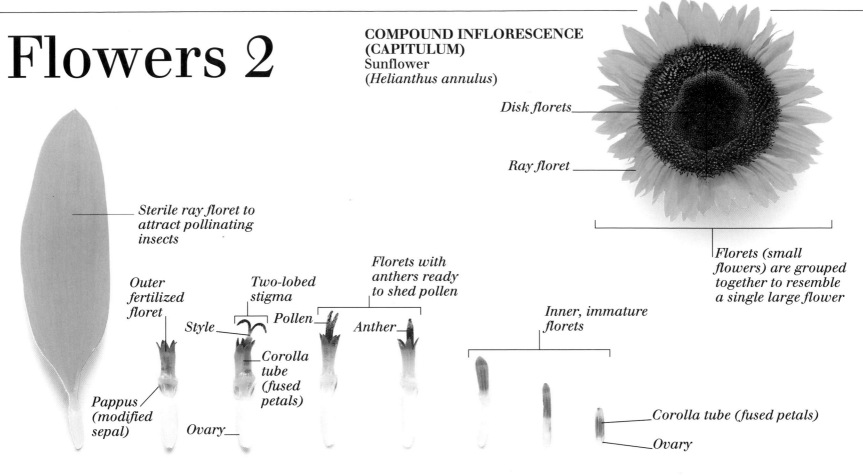

Disk florets

Ray floret

Florets (small
flowers) are grouped
together to resemble
a single large flower

Sterile ray floret to
attract pollinating
insects

Outer
fertilized
floret

Two-lobed
stigma

Florets with
anthers ready
to shed pollen

Style

Pollen

Anther

Inner, immature
florets

Corolla
tube
(fused
petals)

Pappus
(modified
sepal)

Ovary

Corolla tube (fused petals)

Ovary

FLORETS FROM SUNFLOWER

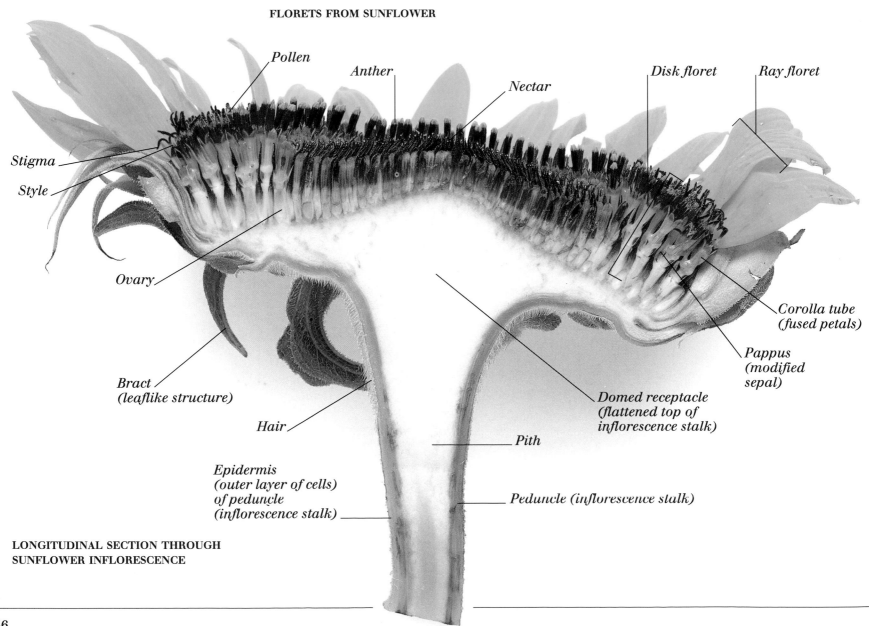

Pollen

Anther

Nectar

Disk floret

Ray floret

Stigma

Style

Ovary

Bract
(leaflike structure)

Hair

Corolla tube
(fused petals)

Pappus
(modified
sepal)

Domed receptacle
(flattened top of
inflorescence stalk)

Pith

Epidermis
(outer layer of cells)
of peduncle
(inflorescence stalk)

Peduncle (inflorescence stalk)

**LONGITUDINAL SECTION THROUGH
SUNFLOWER INFLORESCENCE**

ARRANGEMENT OF FLOWERS ON STEM

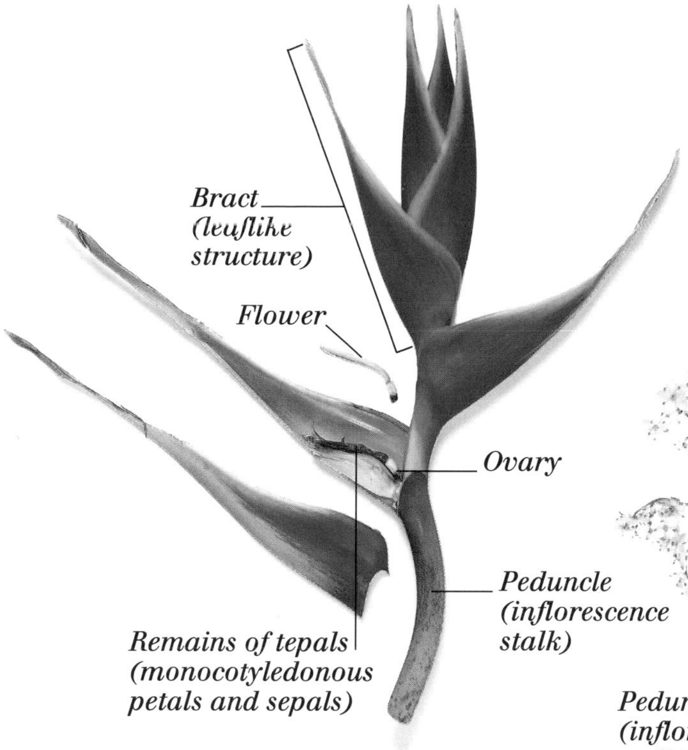

Bract (leaflike structure)

Flower

Ovary

Remains of tepals (monocotyledonous petals and sepals)

Peduncle (inflorescence stalk)

INFLORESCENCE (SPIKE)
Heliconia peruviana

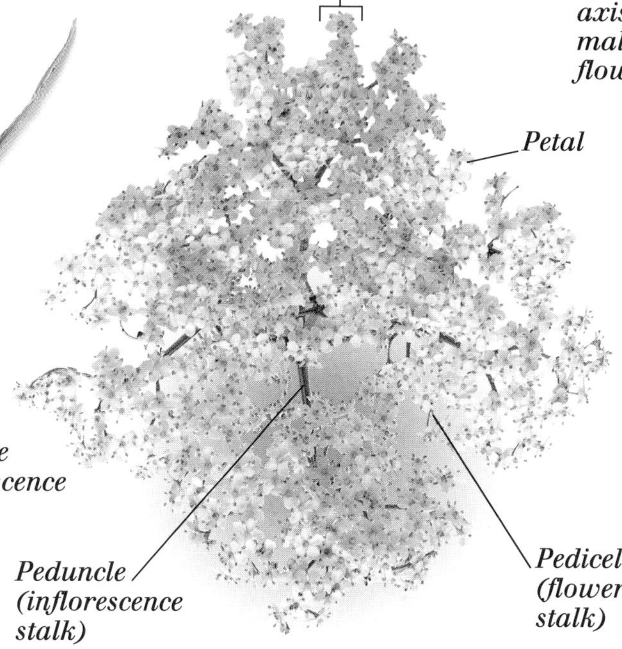

Flower

Petal

Peduncle (inflorescence stalk)

Pedicel (flower stalk)

INFLORESCENCE (COMPOUND UMBEL)
European elder
(*Sambucus nigra*)

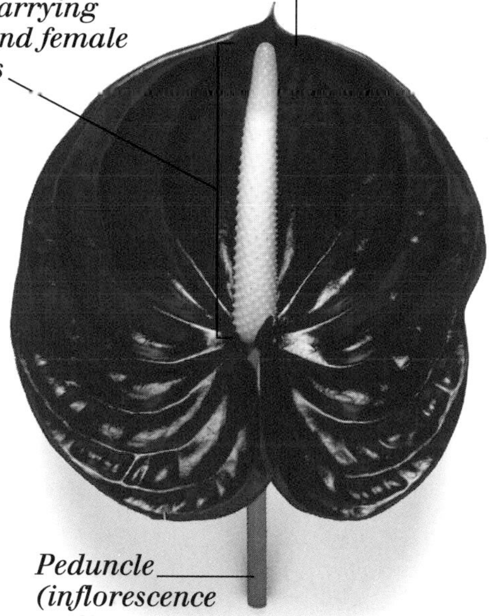

Spathe (large bract) to attract pollinating insects

Spadix (fleshy axis) carrying male and female flowers

Peduncle (inflorescence stalk)

INFLORESCENCE (SPADIX)
Painter's palette
(*Anthurium andreanum*)

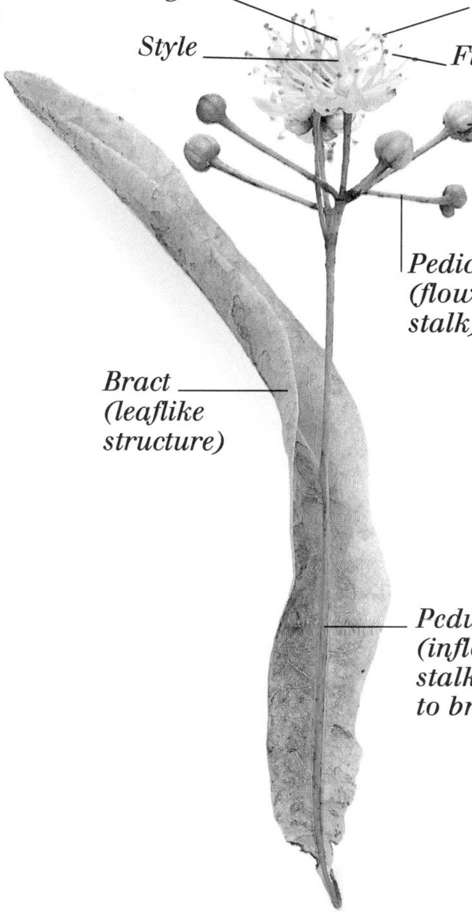

Stigma

Style

Anther

Filament

Stamen

Flower bud

Pedicel (flower stalk)

Bract (leaflike structure)

Peduncle (inflorescence stalk) fused to bract

INFLORESCENCE (DICHASIAL CYME)
Common lime
(*Tilia x europaea*)

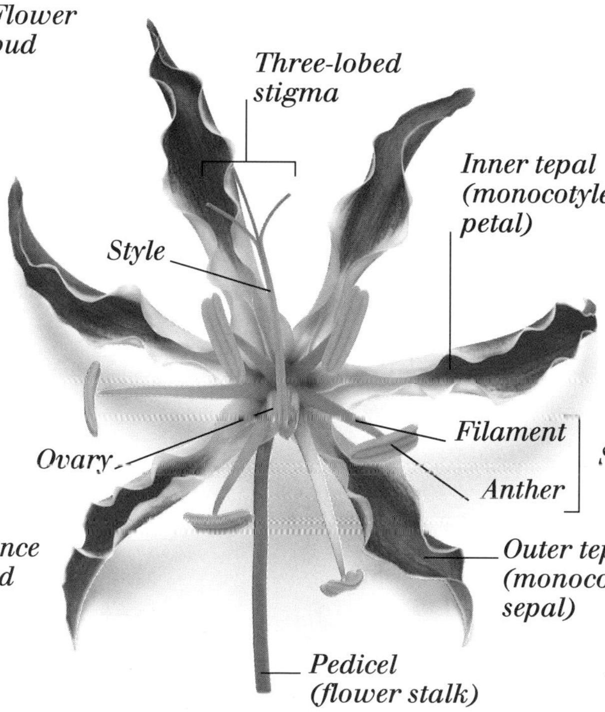

Three-lobed stigma

Style

Ovary

Inner tepal (monocotyledonous petal)

Filament

Stamen

Anther

Outer tepal (monocotyledonous sepal)

Pedicel (flower stalk)

SINGLE FLOWER
Glory lily
(*Gloriosa superba*)

Flower

Peduncle (inflorescence stalk)

Corolla

Calyx

Bract (leaflike structure)

SINGLE FLOWER

INFLORESCENCE (SPHERICAL UMBEL)
Allium sp.

37

Pollination

POLLINATION IS THE TRANSFER OF POLLEN (which contains the male sex cells) from an anther (part of the male reproductive organ) to a stigma (part of the female reproductive organ). This process precedes fertilization (see pp. 40-41). Pollination may occur within the same flower (self-pollination), or between flowers on separate plants of the same species (cross-pollination). In most plants, pollination is carried out either by insects (entomophilous pollination) or by the wind (anemophilous pollination). Less commonly, birds, bats, or water are the agents of pollination. Insect-pollinated flowers are typically scented and brightly colored. They also produce nectar, on which insects feed. Such flowers also tend to have patterns that are visible only in ultraviolet light, which many insects can see but which is invisible to humans. These features attract insects, which become covered with the sticky pollen grains when they visit one flower, and then transfer the pollen to the next flower they visit. Wind-pollinated flowers are generally small, relatively inconspicuous, and unscented. They produce large quantities of light pollen grains that are easily blown by the wind to other flowers.

REPRODUCTIVE STRUCTURES IN WIND-POLLINATED PLANT
Sweet chestnut (*Castanea sativa*)

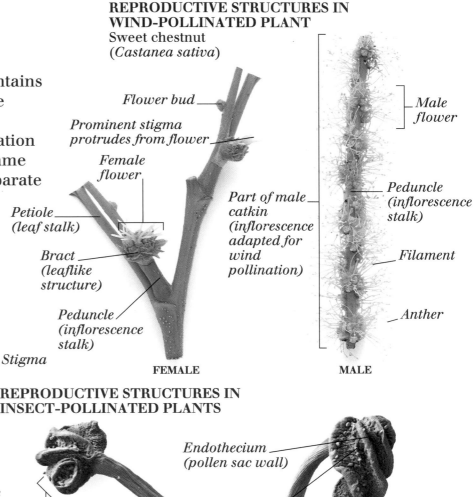

Flower bud

Prominent stigma protrudes from flower

Female flower

Petiole (leaf stalk)

Bract (leaflike structure)

Peduncle (inflorescence stalk)

FEMALE

Male flower

Part of male catkin (inflorescence adapted for wind pollination)

Peduncle (inflorescence stalk)

Filament

Anther

MALE

REPRODUCTIVE STRUCTURES IN INSECT-POLLINATED PLANTS

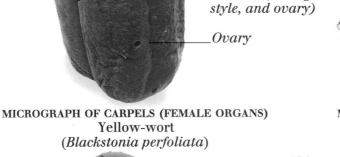

Stigma

Style

Boundary between two fused carpels (each carpel consists of a stigma, style, and ovary)

Ovary

Endothecium (pollen sac wall)

Dehisced (split open) pollen sac

Pollen grain

Anther

Filament

Stamen

Calyx (whorl of sepals)

MICROGRAPH OF CARPELS (FEMALE ORGANS)
Yellow-wort (*Blackstonia perfoliata*)

MICROGRAPH OF STAMENS (MALE ORGANS)
Common centaury (*Centaurium erythraea*)

MICROGRAPHS OF POLLEN GRAINS

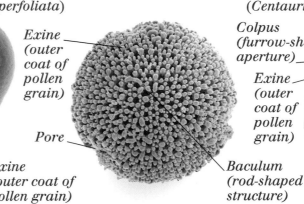

Exine (outer coat of pollen grain)

Pore

EUROPEAN FIELD ELM
(*Ulmus minor*)

Colpus (furrow-shaped aperture)

Exine (outer coat of pollen grain)

JUSTICIA AUREA

Exine (outer coat of pollen grain)

Pore

Baculum (rod-shaped structure)

MEADOW CRANESBILL
(*Geranium pratense*)

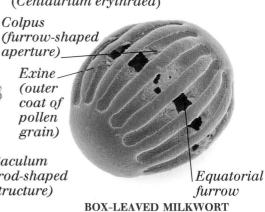

Colpus (furrow-shaped aperture)

Exine (outer coat of pollen grain)

Equatorial furrow

BOX-LEAVED MILKWORT
(*Polygala chamaebuxus*)

INSECT POLLINATION OF MEADOW SAGE

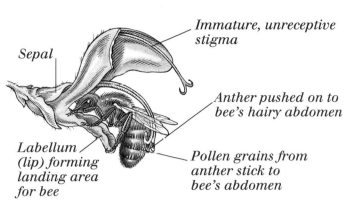

Sepal

Immature, unreceptive stigma

Anther pushed on to bee's hairy abdomen

Labellum (lip) forming landing area for bee

Pollen grains from anther stick to bee's abdomen

1. BEE VISITS FLOWER WITH MATURE ANTHERS BUT IMMATURE STIGMA

Pollen grains attached to hairy abdomen

Long style curves downward when bee enters flower

Mature, receptive stigma touches bee's abdomen, picking up pollen

Sepal

Labellum (lip) forming landing area for bee

2. BEE FLIES TO OTHER FLOWERS

3. BEE VISITS FLOWER WHERE THE ANTHERS HAVE WITHERED AND THE STIGMA IS MATURE

SUNFLOWER UNDER NORMAL AND ULTRAVIOLET LIGHT

Central area of disc florets

Ray floret

NORMAL LIGHT

Petal

Ovary

Stigma

Stamen — [*Filament* / *Anther*]

NORMAL LIGHT

ST JOHN'S WORT UNDER NORMAL AND ULTRAVIOLET LIGHT

Honey guide directs insects to dark, central part of flower

Lighter, outer part of ray floret

Darker, inner part of ray floret

Insects attracted to darkest, central part of flower, which contains nectaries, anthers, and stigmas

Dark central area containing nectaries, anthers, and stigmas

ULTRAVIOLET LIGHT

ULTRAVIOLET LIGHT

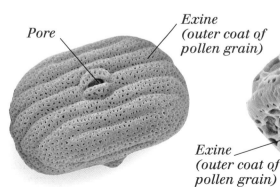

Pore

Exine (outer coat of pollen grain)

Trilete mark (development scar)

Exine (outer coat of pollen grain)

Columella (small column-shaped structure)

Exine (outer coat of pollen grain)

Colpus (furrow-shaped aperture)

Exine (outer coat of pollen grain)

Tricolpate (three colpae) pollen grain

MIMULOPSIS SOLMSII

THESIUM ALPINIUM

RUELLIA GRANDIFLORA

CROSSANDRA NILOTICA

Fertilization

FERTILIZATION IS THE FUSION of male and female
gametes (sex cells) to produce a zygote (embryo).
Following pollination (see pp. 38-39), the pollen
grains that contain the male gametes are on
the stigma, some distance from the female
gamete (ovum) inside the ovule. To enable the
gametes to meet, the pollen grain germinates
and produces a pollen tube, which grows
down and enters the embryo sac (the inner
part of the ovule that contains the ovum).
Two male gametes, traveling at the tip of the
pollen tube, enter the embryo sac. One gamete
fuses with the ovum to produce a zygote that will
develop into an embryo plant. The other male
gamete fuses with two polar nuclei to produce the
endosperm, which acts as a food supply for the
developing embryo. Fertilization also initiates
other changes: the integument (outer part of ovule)
forms a testa (seed coat) around the embryo and
endosperm; the petals fall off; the stigma and style
wither; and the ovary wall forms a layer (called the
pericarp) around the seed. Together, the pericarp
and seed form the fruit, which may be succulent
(see pp. 42-43) or dry (see pp. 44-45). In some
species (such as blackberry), apomixis can occur:
The seed develops without fertilization of the ovum
by a male gamete, but endosperm formation and fruit development
take place as in other species.

BANANA
(Musa 'lacatan')

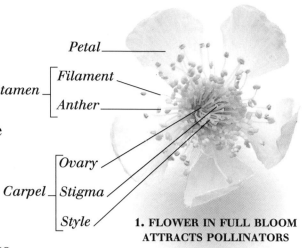

DEVELOPMENT OF A SUCCULENT FRUIT
Blackberry
(Rubus fruticosus)

Petal

Stamen — Filament / Anther

Carpel — Ovary / Stigma / Style

**1. FLOWER IN FULL BLOOM
ATTRACTS POLLINATORS**

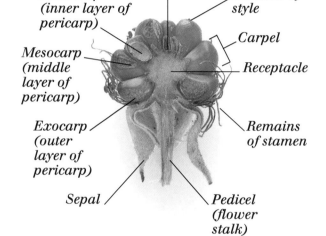

Endocarp
*(inner layer of
pericarp)*

Mesocarp
*(middle
layer of
pericarp)*

Exocarp
*(outer
layer of
pericarp)*

Sepal

Abortive
seed

Remains of
style

Carpel

Receptacle

Remains
of stamen

Pedicel
*(flower
stalk)*

**4. PERICARP FORMS
FLESH, SKIN, AND A HARD INNER
LAYER (SHOWN IN CROSS SECTION)**

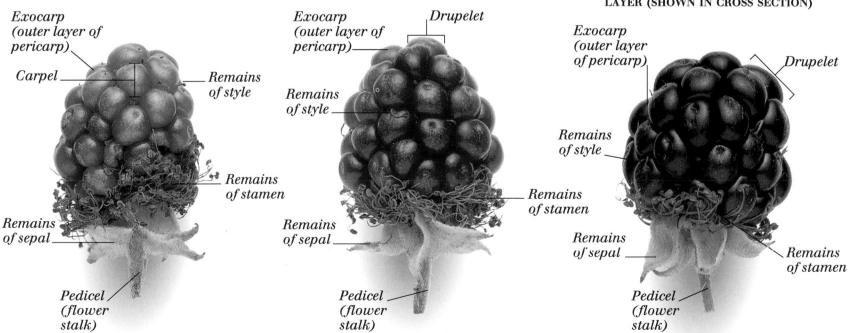

Exocarp
*(outer layer of
pericarp)*

Carpel

Remains
of style

Remains
of stamen

Remains
of sepal

Pedicel
*(flower
stalk)*

**7. MESOCARP (FLESHY PART OF PERICARP)
OF EACH CARPEL STARTS TO
CHANGE COLOR**

Exocarp
*(outer layer of
pericarp)*

Drupelet

Remains
of style

Remains
of stamen

Remains
of sepal

Pedicel
*(flower
stalk)*

**8. CARPELS MATURE INTO DRUPELETS
(SMALL FLESHY FRUITS WITH SINGLE SEEDS
SURROUNDED BY HARD ENDOCARP)**

Exocarp
*(outer layer
of pericarp)*

Drupelet

Remains
of style

Remains
of sepal

Remains
of stamen

Pedicel
*(flower
stalk)*

**9. MESOCARP OF DRUPELET BECOMES
DARKER AND SWEETER**

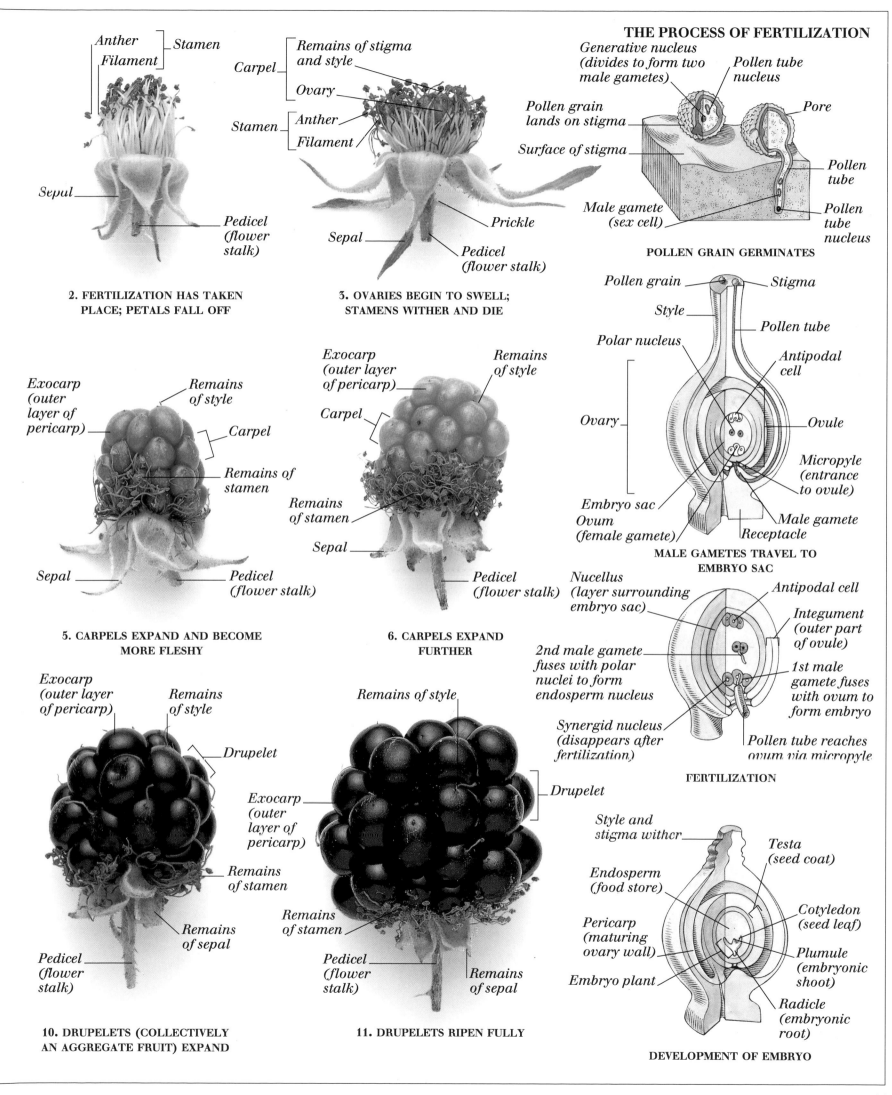

Anther — **Stamen**
Filament

Carpel
Remains of stigma and style
Ovary

Sepal

Stamen
Anther
Filament

Pedicel (flower stalk)

Sepal
Prickle
Pedicel (flower stalk)

2. FERTILIZATION HAS TAKEN PLACE; PETALS FALL OFF

3. OVARIES BEGIN TO SWELL; STAMENS WITHER AND DIE

THE PROCESS OF FERTILIZATION

Generative nucleus (divides to form two male gametes)
Pollen tube nucleus

Pollen grain lands on stigma
Pore

Surface of stigma

Pollen tube

Male gamete (sex cell)
Pollen tube nucleus

POLLEN GRAIN GERMINATES

Exocarp (outer layer of pericarp)
Remains of style

Carpel

Remains of stamen

Sepal
Pedicel (flower stalk)

5. CARPELS EXPAND AND BECOME MORE FLESHY

Exocarp (outer layer of pericarp)
Remains of style

Carpel

Remains of stamen

Sepal

Pedicel (flower stalk)

6. CARPELS EXPAND FURTHER

Pollen grain
Stigma

Style
Pollen tube

Polar nucleus
Antipodal cell

Ovary
Ovule

Micropyle (entrance to ovule)

Embryo sac
Ovum (female gamete)
Male gamete
Receptacle

MALE GAMETES TRAVEL TO EMBRYO SAC

Nucellus (layer surrounding embryo sac)
Antipodal cell

2nd male gamete fuses with polar nuclei to form endosperm nucleus
Integument (outer part of ovule)

1st male gamete fuses with ovum to form embryo

Synergid nucleus (disappears after fertilization)
Pollen tube reaches ovum via micropyle

FERTILIZATION

Exocarp (outer layer of pericarp)
Remains of style

Drupelet

Remains of stamen

Remains of sepal

Pedicel (flower stalk)

10. DRUPELETS (COLLECTIVELY AN AGGREGATE FRUIT) EXPAND

Remains of style

Exocarp (outer layer of pericarp)

Drupelet

Remains of stamen

Pedicel (flower stalk)
Remains of sepal

11. DRUPELETS RIPEN FULLY

Style and stigma wither
Testa (seed coat)

Endosperm (food store)

Pericarp (maturing ovary wall)
Cotyledon (seed leaf)

Plumule (embryonic shoot)

Embryo plant
Radicle (embryonic root)

DEVELOPMENT OF EMBRYO

41

Succulent fruits

A FRUIT IS A FULLY DEVELOPED and ripened ovary—the seed-producing part of a plant's female reproductive organs. Fruits may be succulent or dry (see pp. 44-45). Succulent fruits are fleshy and brightly colored, making them attractive to animals, which eat them and disperse the seeds away from the parent plant. The wall (pericarp) of a succulent fruit has three layers: an outer exocarp, a middle mesocarp, and an inner endocarp. These three layers vary in thickness and texture in different types of fruits and may blend into each other. Succulent fruits can be classed as simple (derived from one ovary) or compound (derived from several ovaries). Simple succulent fruits include berries, which typically have many seeds, and drupes, which typically have a single stone or pit (such as cherry and peach). Compound succulent fruits include aggregate fruits, which are formed from many ovaries in one flower, and multiple fruits, which develop from the ovaries of many flowers. Some fruits, known as false fruits or pseudocarps, develop from parts of the flower in addition to the ovaries. For example, the flesh of the apple is formed from the receptacle (the upper end of the flower stalk).

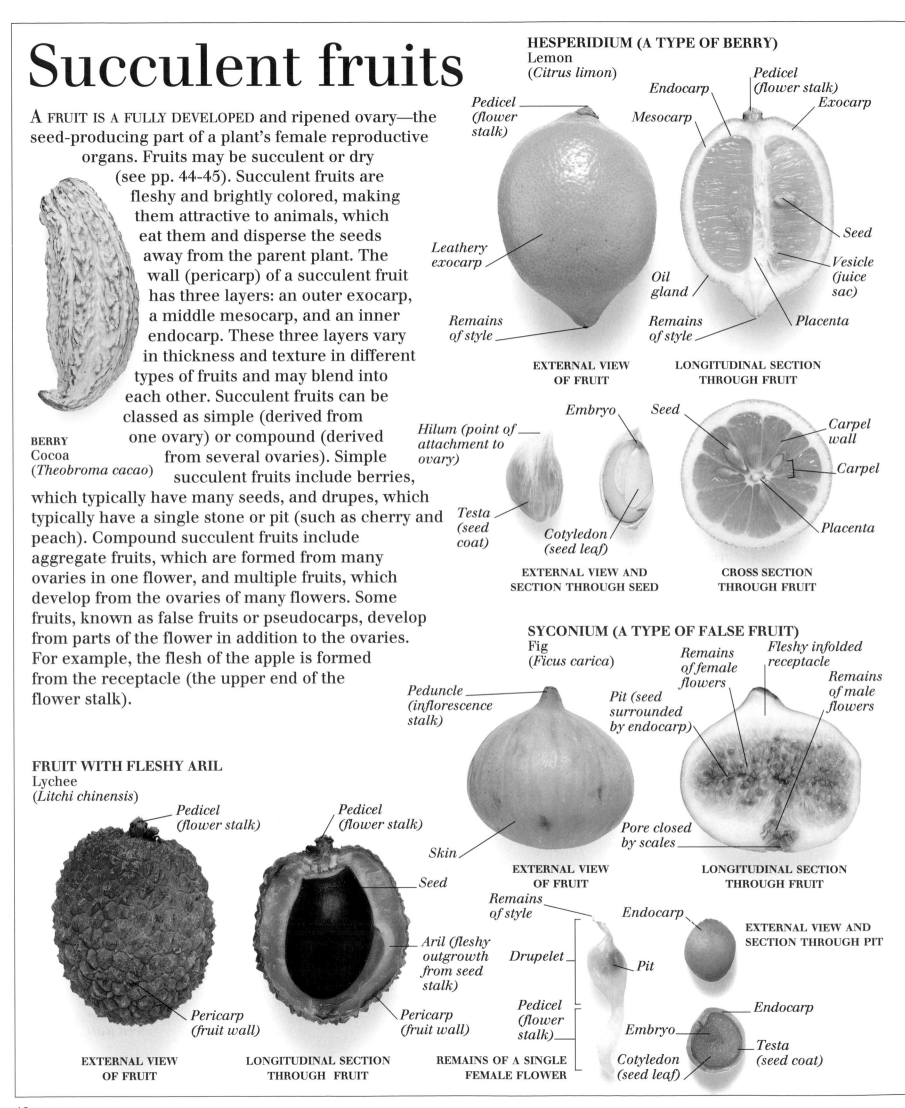

BERRY
Cocoa
(*Theobroma cacao*)

HESPERIDIUM (A TYPE OF BERRY)
Lemon
(*Citrus limon*)

Pedicel (flower stalk)

Endocarp

Pedicel (flower stalk)

Mesocarp

Exocarp

Leathery exocarp

Seed

Oil gland

Vesicle (juice sac)

Remains of style

Remains of style

Placenta

EXTERNAL VIEW OF FRUIT

LONGITUDINAL SECTION THROUGH FRUIT

Embryo

Seed

Carpel wall

Hilum (point of attachment to ovary)

Carpel

Testa (seed coat)

Cotyledon (seed leaf)

Placenta

EXTERNAL VIEW AND SECTION THROUGH SEED

CROSS SECTION THROUGH FRUIT

SYCONIUM (A TYPE OF FALSE FRUIT)
Fig
(*Ficus carica*)

Remains of female flowers

Fleshy infolded receptacle

Peduncle (inflorescence stalk)

Pit (seed surrounded by endocarp)

Remains of male flowers

Skin

Pore closed by scales

FRUIT WITH FLESHY ARIL
Lychee
(*Litchi chinensis*)

Pedicel (flower stalk)

Pedicel (flower stalk)

Seed

EXTERNAL VIEW OF FRUIT

LONGITUDINAL SECTION THROUGH FRUIT

Aril (fleshy outgrowth from seed stalk)

Remains of style

Endocarp

EXTERNAL VIEW AND SECTION THROUGH PIT

Drupelet

Pit

Pericarp (fruit wall)

Pericarp (fruit wall)

Pedicel (flower stalk)

Embryo

Endocarp

Testa (seed coat)

EXTERNAL VIEW OF FRUIT

LONGITUDINAL SECTION THROUGH FRUIT

REMAINS OF A SINGLE FEMALE FLOWER

Cotyledon (seed leaf)

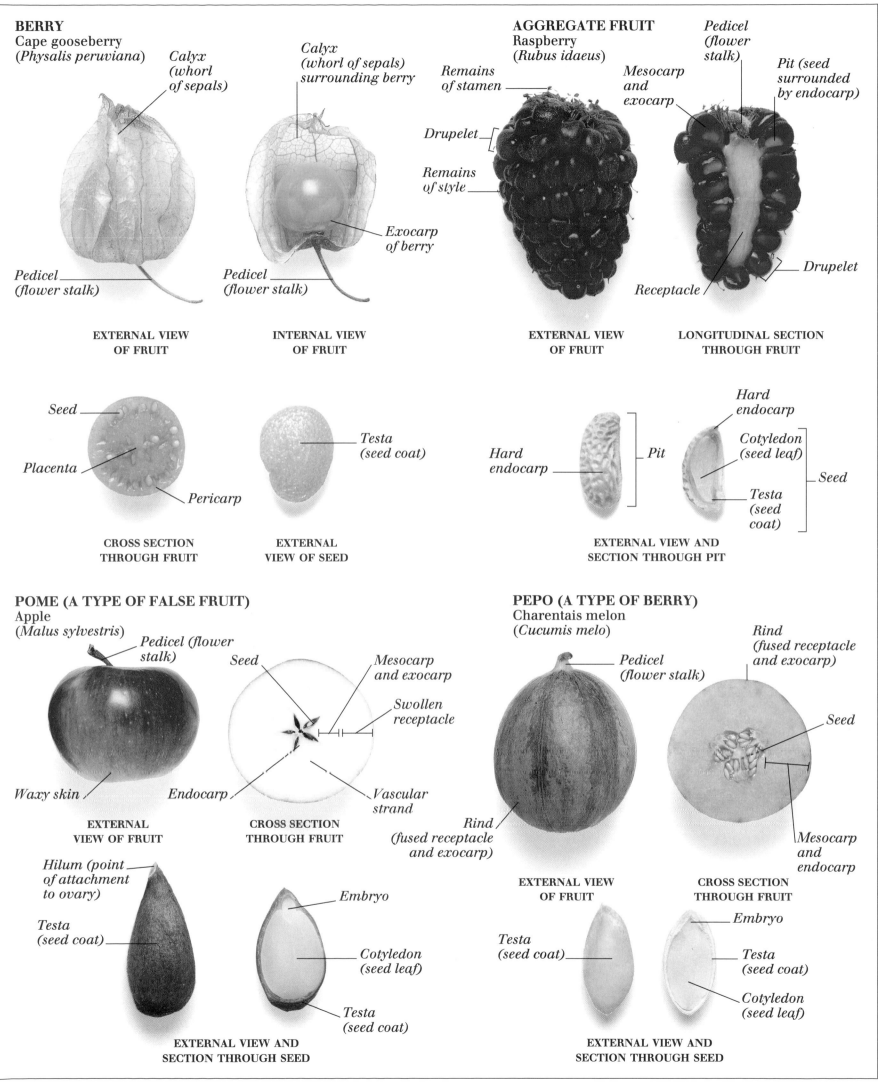

BERRY
Cape gooseberry
(*Physalis peruviana*)

Calyx (whorl of sepals)

Calyx (whorl of sepals) surrounding berry

Pedicel (flower stalk)

Exocarp of berry

Pedicel (flower stalk)

EXTERNAL VIEW OF FRUIT

INTERNAL VIEW OF FRUIT

Seed

Placenta

Testa (seed coat)

Pericarp

CROSS SECTION THROUGH FRUIT

EXTERNAL VIEW OF SEED

AGGREGATE FRUIT
Raspberry
(*Rubus idaeus*)

Remains of stamen

Mesocarp and exocarp

Pedicel (flower stalk)

Pit (seed surrounded by endocarp)

Drupelet

Remains of style

Drupelet

Receptacle

EXTERNAL VIEW OF FRUIT

LONGITUDINAL SECTION THROUGH FRUIT

Hard endocarp

Hard endocarp

Cotyledon (seed leaf)

Pit

Seed

Testa (seed coat)

EXTERNAL VIEW AND SECTION THROUGH PIT

POME (A TYPE OF FALSE FRUIT)
Apple
(*Malus sylvestris*)

Pedicel (flower stalk)

Seed

Mesocarp and exocarp

Swollen receptacle

Waxy skin

Endocarp

Vascular strand

EXTERNAL VIEW OF FRUIT

CROSS SECTION THROUGH FRUIT

Hilum (point of attachment to ovary)

Testa (seed coat)

Embryo

Cotyledon (seed leaf)

Testa (seed coat)

EXTERNAL VIEW AND SECTION THROUGH SEED

PEPO (A TYPE OF BERRY)
Charentais melon
(*Cucumis melo*)

Pedicel (flower stalk)

Rind (fused receptacle and exocarp)

Seed

Rind (fused receptacle and exocarp)

Mesocarp and endocarp

EXTERNAL VIEW OF FRUIT

CROSS SECTION THROUGH FRUIT

Testa (seed coat)

Embryo

Testa (seed coat)

Cotyledon (seed leaf)

EXTERNAL VIEW AND SECTION THROUGH SEED

Dry fruits

DRY FRUITS HAVE A HARD, DRY PERICARP (fruit wall) around their seeds, unlike succulent fruits, which have fleshy pericarps (see pp. 42-43). Dry fruits are divided into three types: dehiscent, in which the pericarp splits open to release the seeds; indehiscent, which do not split open; and schizocarpic, in which the fruit splits but the seeds are not exposed. Dehiscent dry fruits include capsules (for example, love-in-a-mist), follicles (delphinium), legumes (pea), and siliquas (honesty). Typically, the seeds of dehiscent fruits are dispersed by the wind. Indehiscent dry fruits include nuts (sweet chestnut), nutlets (goose grass), achenes (strawberry), caryopses (wheat), samaras (elm), and cypselas (dandelion). Some indehiscent dry fruits are dispersed by the wind, assisted by "wings" (elm) or "parachutes" (dandelion); others (goose grass) have hooked pericarps to aid dispersal on animals' fur. Schizocarpic dry fruits include cremocarps (hogweed), and double samaras (sycamore); these are dispersed by the wind.

NUTLET
Goose grass
(*Galium aparine*)

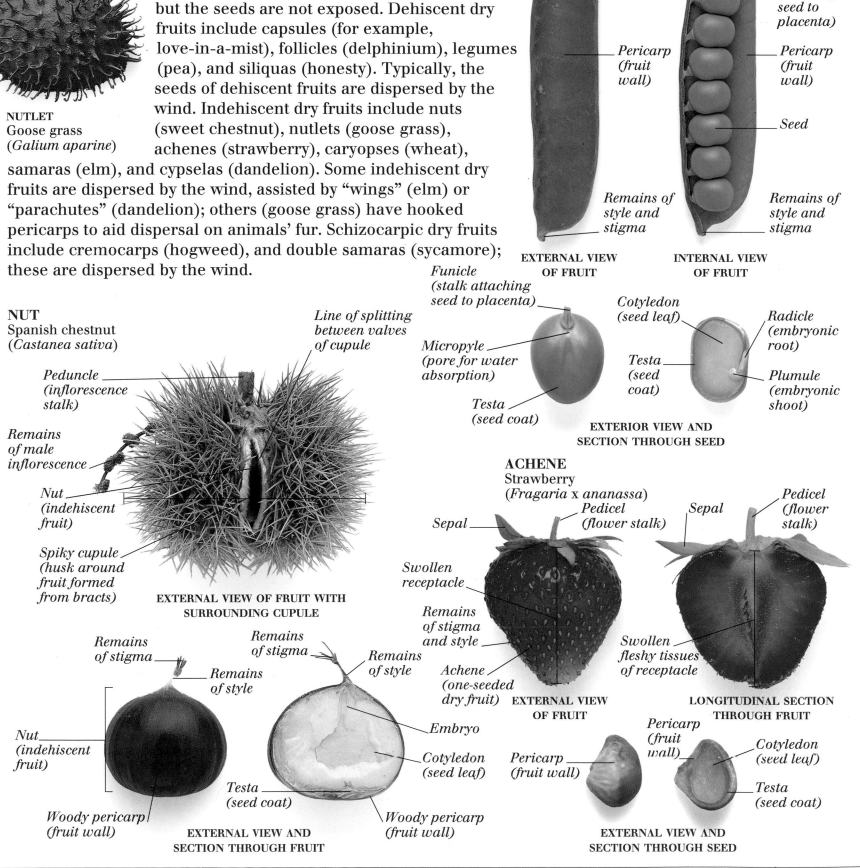

LEGUME
Pea
(*Pisum sativum*)

Pedicel (flower stalk)

Receptacle

Remains of sepal

Remains of stamen

Placenta

Pericarp (fruit wall)

Pedicel (flower stalk)

Receptacle

Remains of sepal

Funicle (stalk attaching seed to placenta)

Pericarp (fruit wall)

Seed

Remains of style and stigma

Remains of style and stigma

EXTERNAL VIEW OF FRUIT

INTERNAL VIEW OF FRUIT

Funicle (stalk attaching seed to placenta)

Micropyle (pore for water absorption)

Testa (seed coat)

Cotyledon (seed leaf)

Radicle (embryonic root)

Testa (seed coat)

Plumule (embryonic shoot)

EXTERIOR VIEW AND SECTION THROUGH SEED

NUT
Spanish chestnut
(*Castanea sativa*)

Line of splitting between valves of cupule

Peduncle (inflorescence stalk)

Remains of male inflorescence

Nut (indehiscent fruit)

Spiky cupule (husk around fruit formed from bracts)

EXTERNAL VIEW OF FRUIT WITH SURROUNDING CUPULE

Remains of stigma

Remains of style

Nut (indehiscent fruit)

Woody pericarp (fruit wall)

EXTERNAL VIEW AND SECTION THROUGH FRUIT

Remains of stigma

Remains of style

Embryo

Cotyledon (seed leaf)

Testa (seed coat)

Woody pericarp (fruit wall)

ACHENE
Strawberry
(*Fragaria* x *ananassa*)

Sepal

Pedicel (flower stalk)

Swollen receptacle

Remains of stigma and style

Achene (one-seeded dry fruit)

EXTERNAL VIEW OF FRUIT

Sepal

Pedicel (flower stalk)

Swollen fleshy tissues of receptacle

LONGITUDINAL SECTION THROUGH FRUIT

Pericarp (fruit wall)

Pericarp (fruit wall)

Cotyledon (seed leaf)

Testa (seed coat)

EXTERNAL VIEW AND SECTION THROUGH SEED

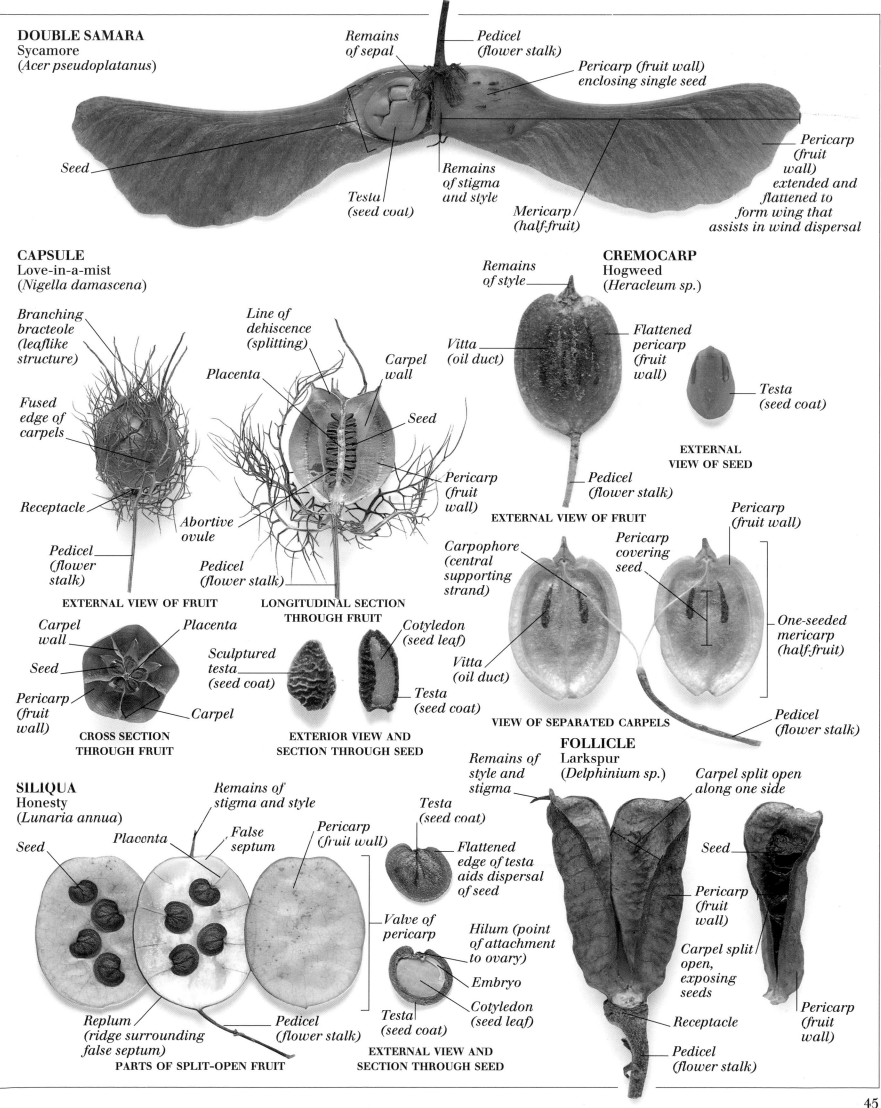

DOUBLE SAMARA
Sycamore
(*Acer pseudoplatanus*)

Remains of sepal

Pedicel (flower stalk)

Pericarp (fruit wall) enclosing single seed

Pericarp (fruit wall) extended and flattened to form wing that assists in wind dispersal

Seed

Remains of stigma and style

Testa (seed coat)

Mericarp (half-fruit)

CAPSULE
Love-in-a-mist
(*Nigella damascena*)

Branching bracteole (leaflike structure)

Fused edge of carpels

Receptacle

Pedicel (flower stalk)

Line of dehiscence (splitting)

Placenta

Carpel wall

Seed

Abortive ovule

Pedicel (flower stalk)

Pericarp (fruit wall)

EXTERNAL VIEW OF FRUIT

LONGITUDINAL SECTION THROUGH FRUIT

Carpel wall

Placenta

Seed

Pericarp (fruit wall)

Carpel

CROSS SECTION THROUGH FRUIT

Sculptured testa (seed coat)

Cotyledon (seed leaf)

Testa (seed coat)

EXTERIOR VIEW AND SECTION THROUGH SEED

CREMOCARP
Hogweed
(*Heracleum sp.*)

Remains of style

Vitta (oil duct)

Flattened pericarp (fruit wall)

Testa (seed coat)

Pedicel (flower stalk)

EXTERNAL VIEW OF SEED

EXTERNAL VIEW OF FRUIT

Carpophore (central supporting strand)

Pericarp covering seed

Pericarp (fruit wall)

Vitta (oil duct)

One-seeded mericarp (half-fruit)

Pedicel (flower stalk)

VIEW OF SEPARATED CARPELS

SILIQUA
Honesty
(*Lunaria annua*)

Seed

Placenta

Remains of stigma and style

False septum

Pericarp (fruit wall)

Replum (ridge surrounding false septum)

Pedicel (flower stalk)

Valve of pericarp

PARTS OF SPLIT-OPEN FRUIT

Testa (seed coat)

Flattened edge of testa aids dispersal of seed

Hilum (point of attachment to ovary)

Embryo

Testa (seed coat)

Cotyledon (seed leaf)

EXTERNAL VIEW AND SECTION THROUGH SEED

FOLLICLE
Larkspur
(*Delphinium sp.*)

Remains of style and stigma

Carpel split open along one side

Seed

Pericarp (fruit wall)

Carpel split open, exposing seeds

Receptacle

Pedicel (flower stalk)

Pericarp (fruit wall)

Germination

GERMINATION IS THE GROWTH OF SEEDS INTO SEEDLINGS. It starts when seeds become active below ground, and ends when the first foliage leaves appear above ground. A seed consists of an embryo and its food supply, surrounded by a testa (seed coat). The embryo is made up of one or two cotyledons (seed leaves) attached to a central axis. The upper part of the axis consists of an epicotyl, which has a plumule (embryonic shoot) at its tip. The lower part of the axis consists of a hypocotyl and a radicle (embryonic root). After dispersal from the parent plant, the seeds dehydrate and enter a period of dormancy. Germination begins, following this dormant period, as long as the seeds have enough water, oxygen, warmth, and, in some cases, light. In the first stages of germination, the seed takes in water; the embryo starts to use its food store; and the radicle swells, breaks through the testa, and grows downward. Germination then proceeds in one of two ways, depending on the type of seed. In epigeal germination, the hypocotyl lengthens, pulling the plumule and its protective cotyledons out of the soil. In hypogeal germination, the cotyledons remain below ground and the epicotyl lengthens, pushing the plumule upward.

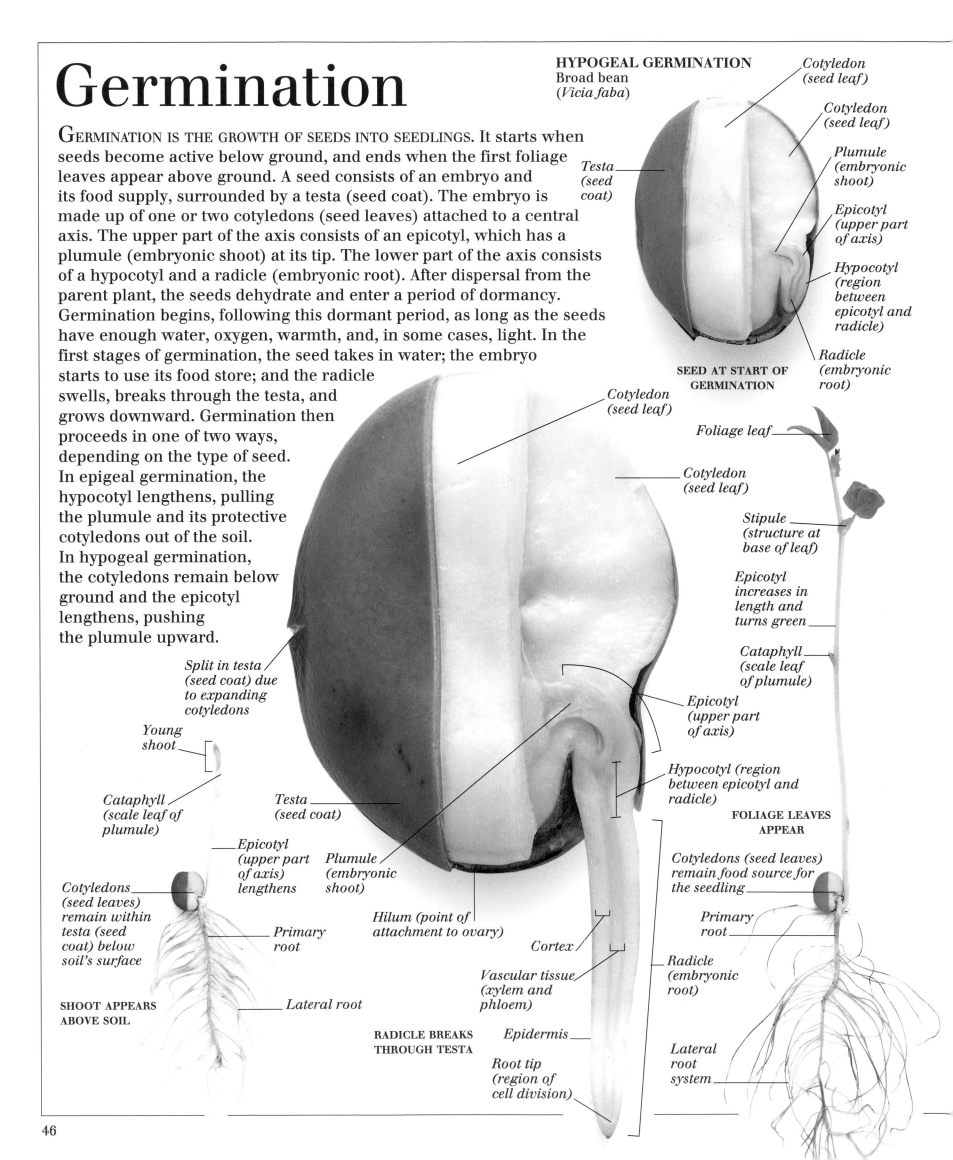

HYPOGEAL GERMINATION
Broad bean (*Vicia faba*)

Cotyledon (seed leaf)

Cotyledon (seed leaf)

Testa (seed coat)

Plumule (embryonic shoot)

Epicotyl (upper part of axis)

Hypocotyl (region between epicotyl and radicle)

Radicle (embryonic root)

SEED AT START OF GERMINATION

Cotyledon (seed leaf)

Cotyledon (seed leaf)

Foliage leaf

Stipule (structure at base of leaf)

Epicotyl increases in length and turns green

Cataphyll (scale leaf of plumule)

Epicotyl (upper part of axis)

Hypocotyl (region between epicotyl and radicle)

FOLIAGE LEAVES APPEAR

Cotyledons (seed leaves) remain food source for the seedling

Primary root

Radicle (embryonic root)

Lateral root system

Split in testa (seed coat) due to expanding cotyledons

Young shoot

Cataphyll (scale leaf of plumule)

Cotyledons (seed leaves) remain within testa (seed coat) below soil's surface

SHOOT APPEARS ABOVE SOIL

Testa (seed coat)

Epicotyl (upper part of axis) lengthens

Plumule (embryonic shoot)

Primary root

Lateral root

Hilum (point of attachment to ovary)

Cortex

Vascular tissue (xylem and phloem)

Epidermis

RADICLE BREAKS THROUGH TESTA

Root tip (region of cell division)

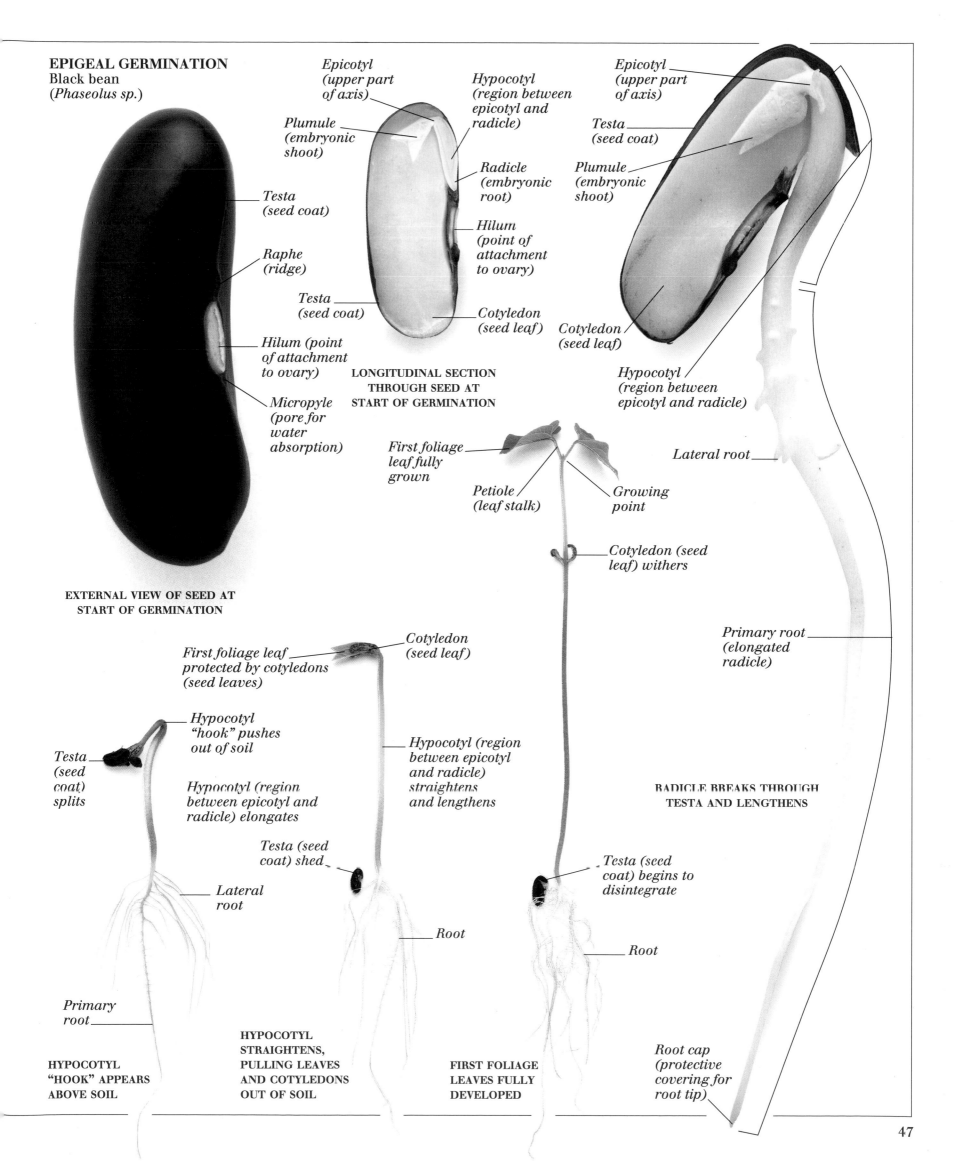

EPIGEAL GERMINATION
Black bean
(*Phaseolus sp.*)

*Testa
(seed coat)*

*Raphe
(ridge)*

*Hilum (point
of attachment
to ovary)*

*Micropyle
(pore for
water
absorption)*

**EXTERNAL VIEW OF SEED AT
START OF GERMINATION**

*Epicotyl
(upper part
of axis)*

*Plumule
(embryonic
shoot)*

*Hypocotyl
(region between
epicotyl and
radicle)*

*Radicle
(embryonic
root)*

*Hilum
(point of
attachment
to ovary)*

*Testa
(seed coat)*

*Cotyledon
(seed leaf)*

**LONGITUDINAL SECTION
THROUGH SEED AT
START OF GERMINATION**

*Epicotyl
(upper part
of axis)*

*Testa
(seed coat)*

*Plumule
(embryonic
shoot)*

*Cotyledon
(seed leaf)*

*Hypocotyl
(region between
epicotyl and radicle)*

*First foliage
leaf fully
grown*

*Petiole
(leaf stalk)*

*Growing
point*

*Cotyledon (seed
leaf) withers*

Lateral root

*Primary root
(elongated
radicle)*

*First foliage leaf
protected by cotyledons
(seed leaves)*

*Cotyledon
(seed leaf)*

*Hypocotyl
"hook" pushes
out of soil*

*Testa
(seed
coat)
splits*

*Hypocotyl (region
between epicotyl and
radicle) elongates*

*Testa (seed
coat) shed*

*Lateral
root*

*Hypocotyl (region
between epicotyl
and radicle)
straightens
and lengthens*

Root

**RADICLE BREAKS THROUGH
TESTA AND LENGTHENS**

*Testa (seed
coat) begins to
disintegrate*

Root

*Primary
root*

**HYPOCOTYL
"HOOK" APPEARS
ABOVE SOIL**

**HYPOCOTYL
STRAIGHTENS,
PULLING LEAVES
AND COTYLEDONS
OUT OF SOIL**

**FIRST FOLIAGE
LEAVES FULLY
DEVELOPED**

*Root cap
(protective
covering for
root tip)*

47

Vegetative reproduction

MANY PLANTS CAN PROPAGATE THEMSELVES by vegetative reproduction. In this process, part of a plant separates, takes root, and grows into a new plant. Vegetative reproduction is a type of asexual reproduction; it involves only one parent and there is no fusion of gametes (sex cells). Plants use various structures to reproduce vegetatively. Some plants use underground storage organs. Such organs include rhizomes (horizontal, underground stems), the branches of which produce new plants; bulbs (swollen leaf bases) and corms (swollen stems), which produce daughter bulbs or corms that separate from the parent; and stem tubers (thickened underground stems) and root tubers (swollen adventitious roots), which also separate from the parent. Other propagative structures include runners and stolons, creeping horizontal stems that take root and produce new plants; bulbils, small bulbs that develop on the stem or in the place of flowers, and then drop off and grow into new plants; and adventitious buds, miniature plants that form on leaf margins before dropping to the ground and growing into mature plants.

CORM
Gladiolus
(*Gladiolus sp.*)

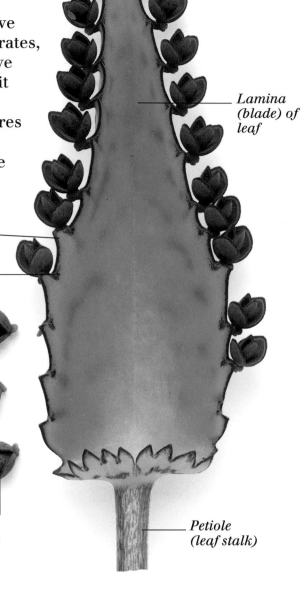

ADVENTITIOUS BUD
Mexican hat plant
(*Kalanchoe daigremontiana*)

Apex of leaf

Lamina (blade) of leaf

Leaf margin

Notch in leaf margin containing meristematic (actively dividing) cells

Adventitious bud (detachable bud with adventitious roots) drops from leaf

Petiole (leaf stalk)

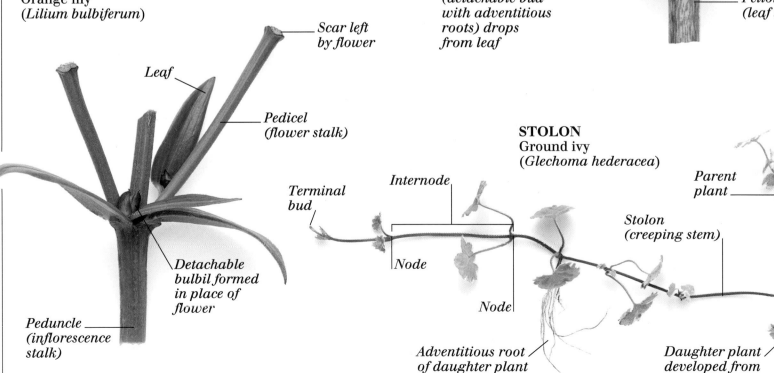

BULBIL IN PLACE OF FLOWER
Orange lily
(*Lilium bulbiferum*)

Scar left by flower

Leaf

Pedicel (flower stalk)

Detachable bulbil formed in place of flower

Peduncle (inflorescence stalk)

STOLON
Ground ivy
(*Glechoma hederacea*)

Terminal bud

Internode

Node

Node

Parent plant

Stolon (creeping stem)

Adventitious root of daughter plant

Daughter plant developed from lateral bud

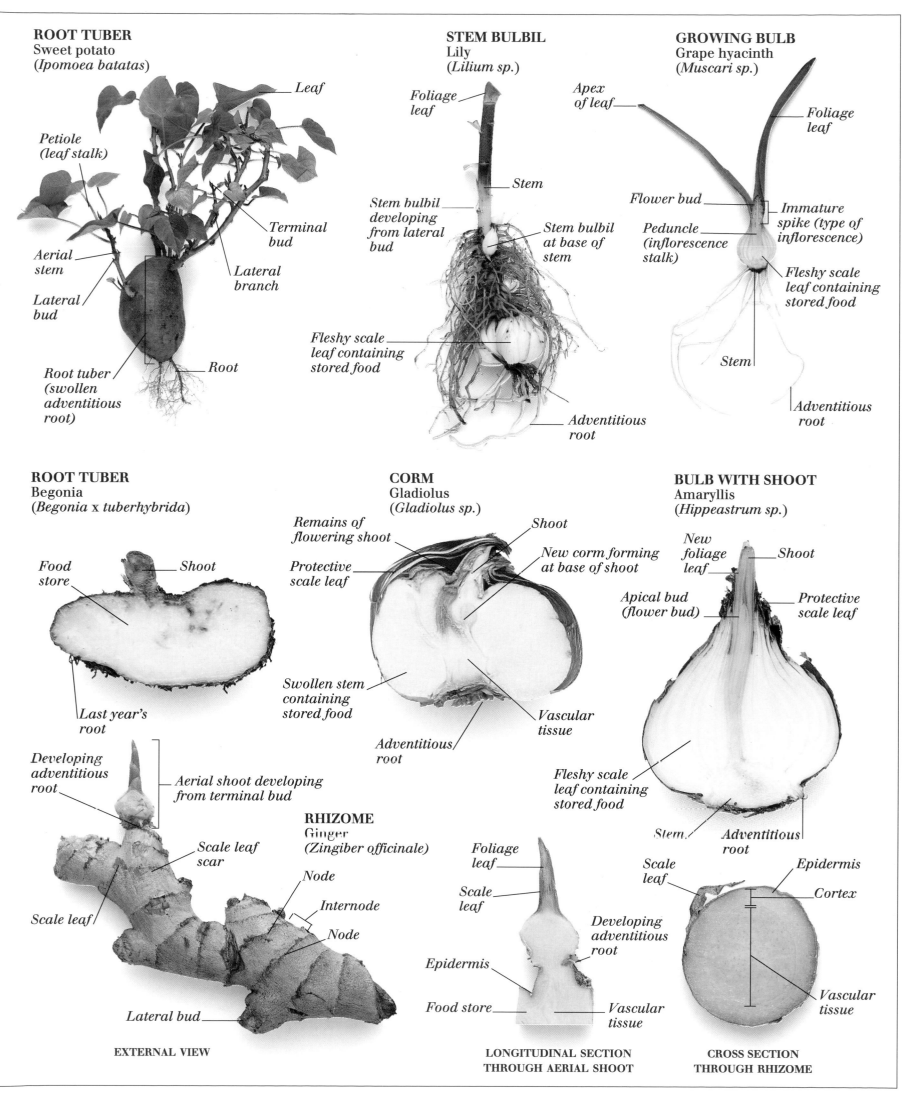

ROOT TUBER
Sweet potato
(*Ipomoea batatas*)

Leaf

Petiole
(leaf stalk)

Terminal
bud

Aerial
stem

Lateral
branch

Lateral
bud

Root tuber
(swollen
adventitious
root)

Root

STEM BULBIL
Lily
(*Lilium sp.*)

Foliage
leaf

Stem

Stem bulbil
developing
from lateral
bud

Stem bulbil
at base of
stem

Fleshy scale
leaf containing
stored food

Adventitious
root

GROWING BULB
Grape hyacinth
(*Muscari sp.*)

Apex
of leaf

Foliage
leaf

Flower bud

Immature
spike (type of
inflorescence)

Peduncle
(inflorescence
stalk)

Fleshy scale
leaf containing
stored food

Stem

Adventitious
root

ROOT TUBER
Begonia
(*Begonia* x *tuberhybrida*)

Food
store

Shoot

Last year's
root

Developing
adventitious
root

Aerial shoot developing
from terminal bud

Scale leaf
scar

Scale leaf

Lateral bud

EXTERNAL VIEW

CORM
Gladiolus
(*Gladiolus sp.*)

Remains of
flowering shoot

Shoot

Protective
scale leaf

New corm forming
at base of shoot

Swollen stem
containing
stored food

Adventitious
root

Vascular
tissue

RHIZOME
Ginger
(*Zingiber officinale*)

Node

Internode

Node

Foliage
leaf

Scale
leaf

Developing
adventitious
root

Epidermis

Food store

Vascular
tissue

LONGITUDINAL SECTION
THROUGH AERIAL SHOOT

BULB WITH SHOOT
Amaryllis
(*Hippeastrum sp.*)

New
foliage
leaf

Shoot

Apical bud
(flower bud)

Protective
scale leaf

Fleshy scale
leaf containing
stored food

Stem

Adventitious
root

Scale
leaf

Epidermis

Cortex

Vascular
tissue

CROSS SECTION
THROUGH RHIZOME

Dryland plants

DRYLAND PLANTS (XEROPHYTES) are able to survive in unfavorable habitats. All are found in places where little water is available; some live in high temperatures that cause excessive loss of water from the leaves. Xerophytes show a number of adaptations to dry conditions. These include reduced leaf area, rolled leaves, sunken stomata, hairs, spines, and thick cuticles. One group, succulent plants, stores water in specially enlarged spongy tissues found in leaves, roots, or stems. Leaf succulents have enlarged, fleshy, water-storing leaves. Root succulents have a large underground water-storage organ with short-lived stems and leaves above ground. Stem succulents are represented by the cacti (family Cactaceae). Cacti stems are fleshy, green, and photosynthetic. They are typically ribbed or covered by tubercles in rows, with leaves being reduced to spines or entirely absent.

LEAF SUCCULENT *Lithops sp.*

STEM SUCCULENT
Golden barrel cactus
(*Echinocactus grusonii*)

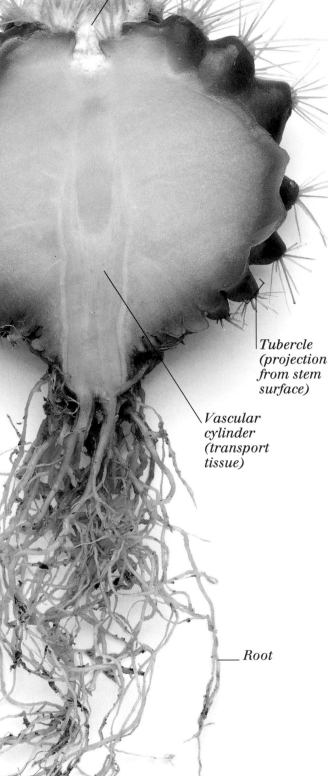

Areole (modified lateral shoot)

Trichome (hair)

Spine (modified leaf)

Waxy cuticle (waterproof covering)

Water-storing parenchyma (packing tissue)

Tubercle (projection from stem surface)

Vascular cylinder (transport tissue)

Root

LONGITUDINAL SECTION THROUGH STEM

Spine (modified leaf)

Tubercle (projection from stem surface)

Root

EXTERNAL VIEW

Sinuous (wavy) cell wall

Stoma (pore) controlling exchange of gases

MICROGRAPH OF STEM SURFACE

Spine (modified leaf)

Areole (modified lateral shoot)

Tubercle (projection from stem surface)

Waxy cuticle (waterproof covering)

DETAIL OF STEM SURFACE

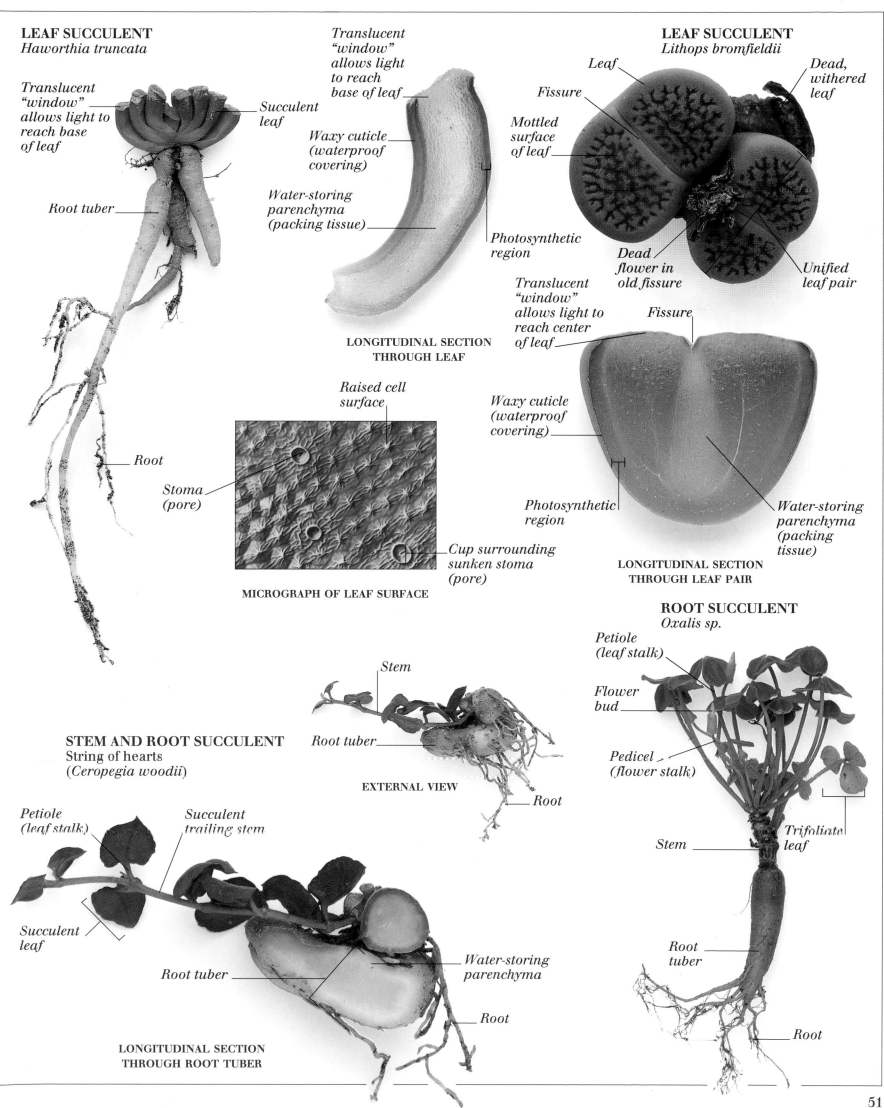

LEAF SUCCULENT
Haworthia truncata

Translucent "window" allows light to reach base of leaf

Succulent leaf

Root tuber

Root

Translucent "window" allows light to reach base of leaf

Waxy cuticle (waterproof covering)

Water-storing parenchyma (packing tissue)

Photosynthetic region

LONGITUDINAL SECTION THROUGH LEAF

Raised cell surface

Stoma (pore)

Cup surrounding sunken stoma (pore)

MICROGRAPH OF LEAF SURFACE

LEAF SUCCULENT
Lithops bromfieldii

Leaf

Fissure

Mottled surface of leaf

Dead, withered leaf

Dead flower in old fissure

Unified leaf pair

Translucent "window" allows light to reach center of leaf

Fissure

Waxy cuticle (waterproof covering)

Photosynthetic region

Water-storing parenchyma (packing tissue)

LONGITUDINAL SECTION THROUGH LEAF PAIR

ROOT SUCCULENT
Oxalis sp.

Petiole (leaf stalk)

Flower bud

Pedicel (flower stalk)

Trifoliate leaf

Stem

Root tuber

Root

Stem

Root tuber

Root

EXTERNAL VIEW

STEM AND ROOT SUCCULENT
String of hearts
(*Ceropegia woodii*)

Petiole (leaf stalk)

Succulent trailing stem

Succulent leaf

Root tuber

Water-storing parenchyma

Root

LONGITUDINAL SECTION THROUGH ROOT TUBER

Wetland plants

WETLAND PLANTS GROW SUBMERGED IN WATER, either partially, like the water hyacinth, or completely, like the pondweeds, and show various adaptations to this habitat. Typically, there are numerous air spaces inside the stems, leaves, and roots; these aid gas exchange and buoyancy. Submerged parts generally have no cuticle (waterproof covering), allowing the plants to absorb minerals and gases directly from the water. Also, because they are supported by the water, wetland plants need little of the supportive tissue found in land plants. Stomata, the gas exchange pores, are absent from plants that are completely submerged. In partially submerged plants with floating leaves, such as water lilies, stomata are found on the upper leaf surfaces, where they cannot be flooded.

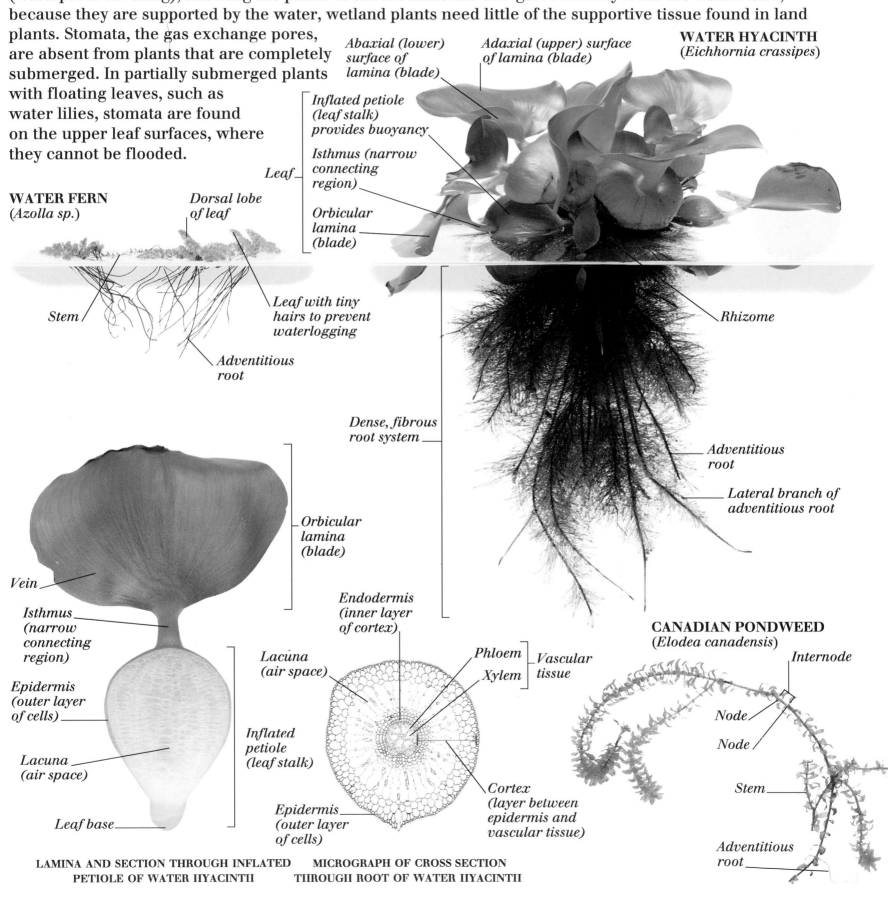

WATER FERN
(*Azolla sp.*)

Dorsal lobe of leaf

Stem

Leaf with tiny hairs to prevent waterlogging

Adventitious root

WATER HYACINTH
(*Eichhornia crassipes*)

Abaxial (lower) surface of lamina (blade)

Adaxial (upper) surface of lamina (blade)

Inflated petiole (leaf stalk) provides buoyancy

Isthmus (narrow connecting region)

Leaf

Orbicular lamina (blade)

Rhizome

Dense, fibrous root system

Adventitious root

Lateral branch of adventitious root

Orbicular lamina (blade)

Vein

Isthmus (narrow connecting region)

Epidermis (outer layer of cells)

Lacuna (air space)

Leaf base

Lacuna (air space)

Inflated petiole (leaf stalk)

Endodermis (inner layer of cortex)

Phloem

Xylem

Vascular tissue

Epidermis (outer layer of cells)

Cortex (layer between epidermis and vascular tissue)

CANADIAN PONDWEED
(*Elodea canadensis*)

Internode

Node

Node

Stem

Adventitious root

LAMINA AND SECTION THROUGH INFLATED PETIOLE OF WATER HYACINTH

MICROGRAPH OF CROSS SECTION THROUGH ROOT OF WATER HYACINTH

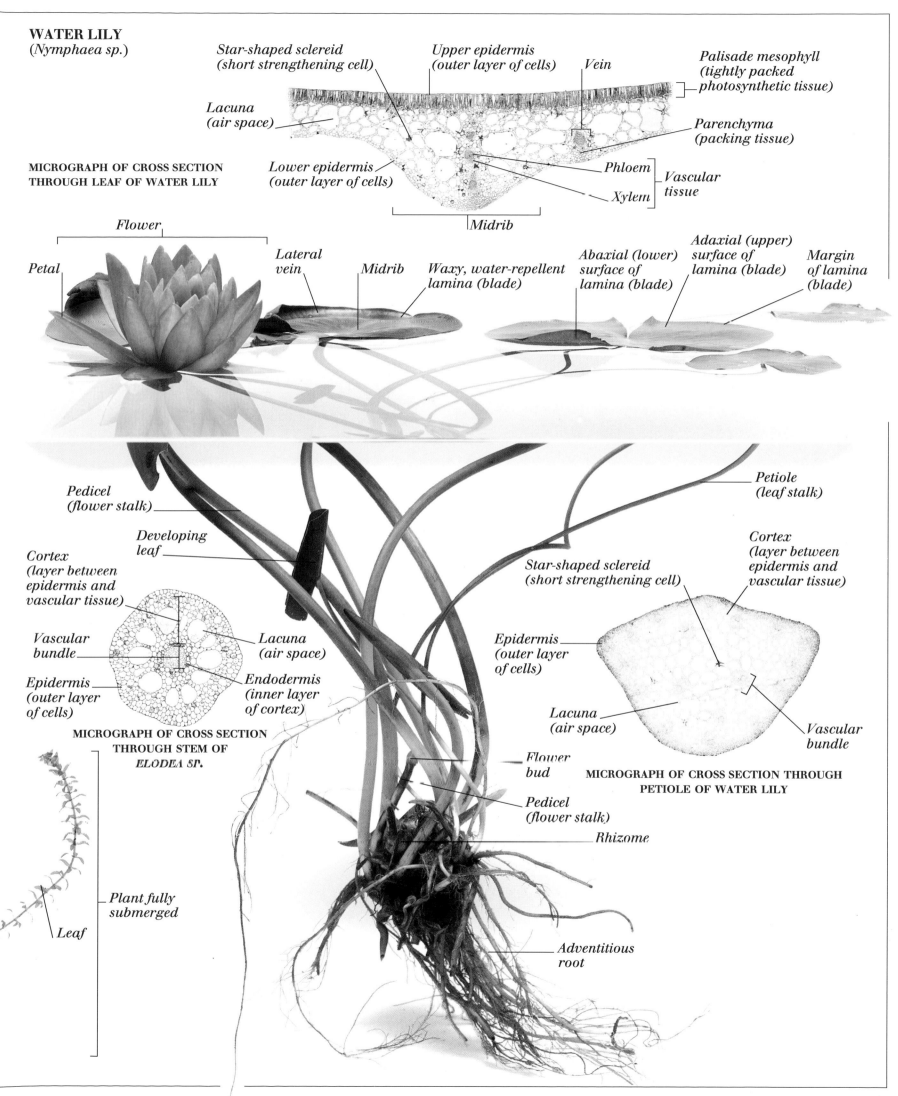

WATER LILY
(*Nymphaea sp.*)

Star-shaped sclereid (short strengthening cell)

Upper epidermis (outer layer of cells)

Vein

Palisade mesophyll (tightly packed photosynthetic tissue)

Lacuna (air space)

MICROGRAPH OF CROSS SECTION THROUGH LEAF OF WATER LILY

Lower epidermis (outer layer of cells)

Parenchyma (packing tissue)

Phloem

Xylem

Vascular tissue

Midrib

Flower

Petal

Lateral vein

Midrib

Waxy, water-repellent lamina (blade)

Abaxial (lower) surface of lamina (blade)

Adaxial (upper) surface of lamina (blade)

Margin of lamina (blade)

Pedicel (flower stalk)

Petiole (leaf stalk)

Developing leaf

Cortex (layer between epidermis and vascular tissue)

Cortex (layer between epidermis and vascular tissue)

Star-shaped sclereid (short strengthening cell)

Vascular bundle

Lacuna (air space)

Epidermis (outer layer of cells)

Epidermis (outer layer of cells)

Endodermis (inner layer of cortex)

Lacuna (air space)

Vascular bundle

MICROGRAPH OF CROSS SECTION THROUGH STEM OF *ELODEA SP.*

MICROGRAPH OF CROSS SECTION THROUGH PETIOLE OF WATER LILY

Flower bud

Pedicel (flower stalk)

Rhizome

Plant fully submerged

Leaf

Adventitious root

53

Carnivorous plants

CARNIVOROUS (INSECTIVOROUS) PLANTS FEED ON INSECTS and other small animals in addition to producing food in their leaves by photosynthesis. The nutrients absorbed from trapped insects allow carnivorous plants to thrive in acid, boggy soils that lack essential minerals, especially nitrates, where most other plants could not survive. All carnivorous plants have some leaves modified as traps. Many use bright colors and scented nectar to attract prey, and most use enzymes to digest the prey. There are three types of traps. Pitcher plants, such as the monkey cup and cobra lily, have leaves modified as pitcher-shaped pitfall traps, half-filled with water. Once lured inside the mouth of the trap, insects lose their footing on the slippery surface, fall into the liquid, and either decompose or are digested. Venus fly-traps use a spring-trap mechanism; when an insect touches trigger hairs on the inner surfaces of the leaves, the two lobes of the trap snap shut. Butterworts and sundews entangle prey by sticky droplets on the leaf surface, while the edges of the leaves slowly curl over to envelop and digest the prey.

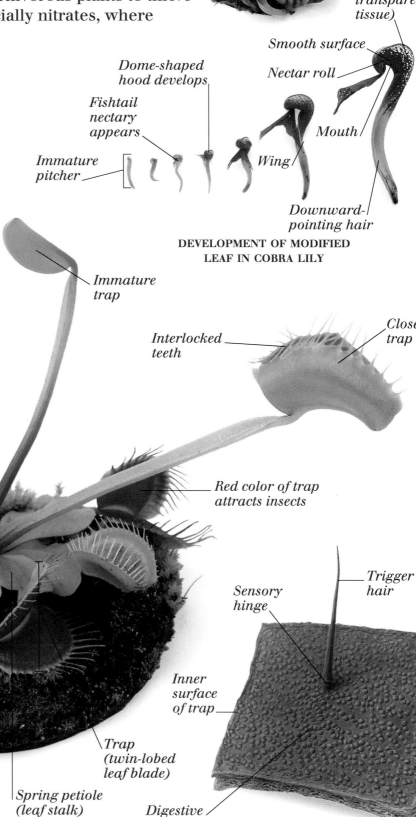

A PITCHER PLANT
Cobra lily (*Darlingtonia californica*)

Areola ("window" of transparent tissue)
Fishtail nectary
Hood
Wing
Pitcher
Tubular petiole (leaf stalk)
Areola ("window" of transparent tissue)

Smooth surface
Nectar roll
Dome-shaped hood develops
Fishtail nectary appears
Mouth
Immature pitcher
Wing
Downward-pointing hair

DEVELOPMENT OF MODIFIED LEAF IN COBRA LILY

Immature trap

Interlocked teeth
Closed trap

Red color of trap attracts insects

VENUS FLYTRAP
(*Dionaea muscipula*)

Phyllode (flattened petiole)

Summer petiole (leaf stalk)

Nectary zone (glands secrete nectar)

Digestive zone (glands secrete digestive enzymes)

Tooth

Lobe of trap

Midrib (hinge of trap)

Trigger hair

Trap (twin-lobed leaf blade)

Spring petiole (leaf stalk)

Trigger hair
Sensory hinge
Inner surface of trap
Digestive gland

MICROGRAPH OF LOBE OF VENUS FLYTRAP

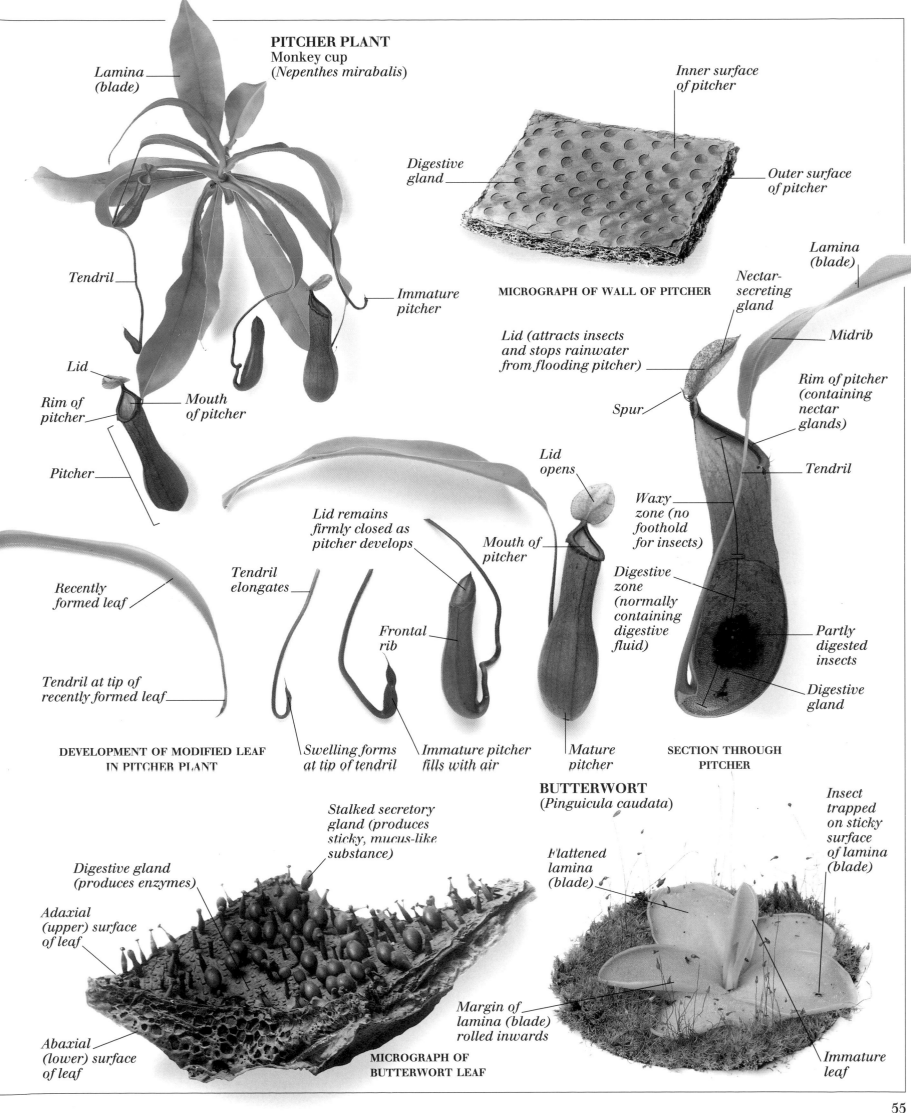

PITCHER PLANT
Monkey cup
(*Nepenthes mirabalis*)

Lamina (blade)

Tendril

Immature pitcher

Lid

Rim of pitcher

Mouth of pitcher

Pitcher

Inner surface of pitcher

Digestive gland

Outer surface of pitcher

MICROGRAPH OF WALL OF PITCHER

Lamina (blade)

Nectar-secreting gland

Midrib

Lid (attracts insects and stops rainwater from flooding pitcher)

Rim of pitcher (containing nectar glands)

Spur

Tendril

Waxy zone (no foothold for insects)

Digestive zone (normally containing digestive fluid)

Partly digested insects

Digestive gland

Recently formed leaf

Tendril elongates

Lid remains firmly closed as pitcher develops

Lid opens

Mouth of pitcher

Tendril at tip of recently formed leaf

Frontal rib

DEVELOPMENT OF MODIFIED LEAF IN PITCHER PLANT

Swelling forms at tip of tendril

Immature pitcher fills with air

Mature pitcher

SECTION THROUGH PITCHER

BUTTERWORT
(*Pinguicula caudata*)

Stalked secretory gland (produces sticky, mucus-like substance)

Insect trapped on sticky surface of lamina (blade)

Digestive gland (produces enzymes)

Flattened lamina (blade)

Adaxial (upper) surface of leaf

Margin of lamina (blade) rolled inwards

Abaxial (lower) surface of leaf

MICROGRAPH OF BUTTERWORT LEAF

Immature leaf

55

Epiphytic and parasitic plants

EPIPHYTIC AND PARASITIC PLANTS GROW ON OTHER LIVING PLANTS. Typically, epiphytic plants are not rooted in the soil. Instead, they live above ground level on the stems and branches of other plants. Epiphytes obtain water from trapped rainwater and from moisture in the air. They obtain minerals from organic matter that has accumulated on the surface of the plant on which they are growing. Like other green plants, epiphytes produce their food by photosynthesis. Epiphytes include tropical orchids and bromeliads (air plants) and some mosses that live in temperate regions. Parasitic plants obtain all their nutrient requirements from the host plants on which they grow. The parasites produce haustoria, root-like organs that penetrate the stem or roots of the host and grow inward to merge with the host's vascular tissue. These extract water, minerals, and manufactured nutrients. Because they have no need to produce their own food, parasitic plants lack chlorophyll, the green photosynthetic pigment, and they have no foliage leaves. Partial parasitic plants, like mistletoe, obtain water and minerals from the host plant but have green leaves and stems and are therefore able to produce their own food by photosynthesis.

EPIPHYTIC BROMELIAD
Aechmea miniata

Inflorescence (spike)

Peduncle (inflorescence stalk)

Flower bud

Strap-shaped arching leaf (part of rosette of leaves)

Leaf margin with spines

Overlapping leaf bases in which rainwater is trapped

Mass of adventitious roots

Stem

Bark of tree to which epiphyte is attached

EPIPHYTIC ORCHID
Brassavola nodosa

Peduncle (inflorescence stalk)

Pedicel (flower stalk)

Flower

Scale leaf

Leaf

Velamen (multilayered epidermis capable of absorbing water from rain or condensation)

Exodermis (outer layer of cortex)

Cortex (layer between epidermis and vascular tissue)

Cortex cell containing chloroplasts

Pith

Aerial root

Vascular tissue — Xylem / Phloem

Endodermis (inner layer of cortex)

Node

Stem

Bark of tree to which epiphyte is attached

MICROGRAPH OF CROSS SECTION THROUGH AERIAL ROOT OF EPIPHYTIC ORCHID

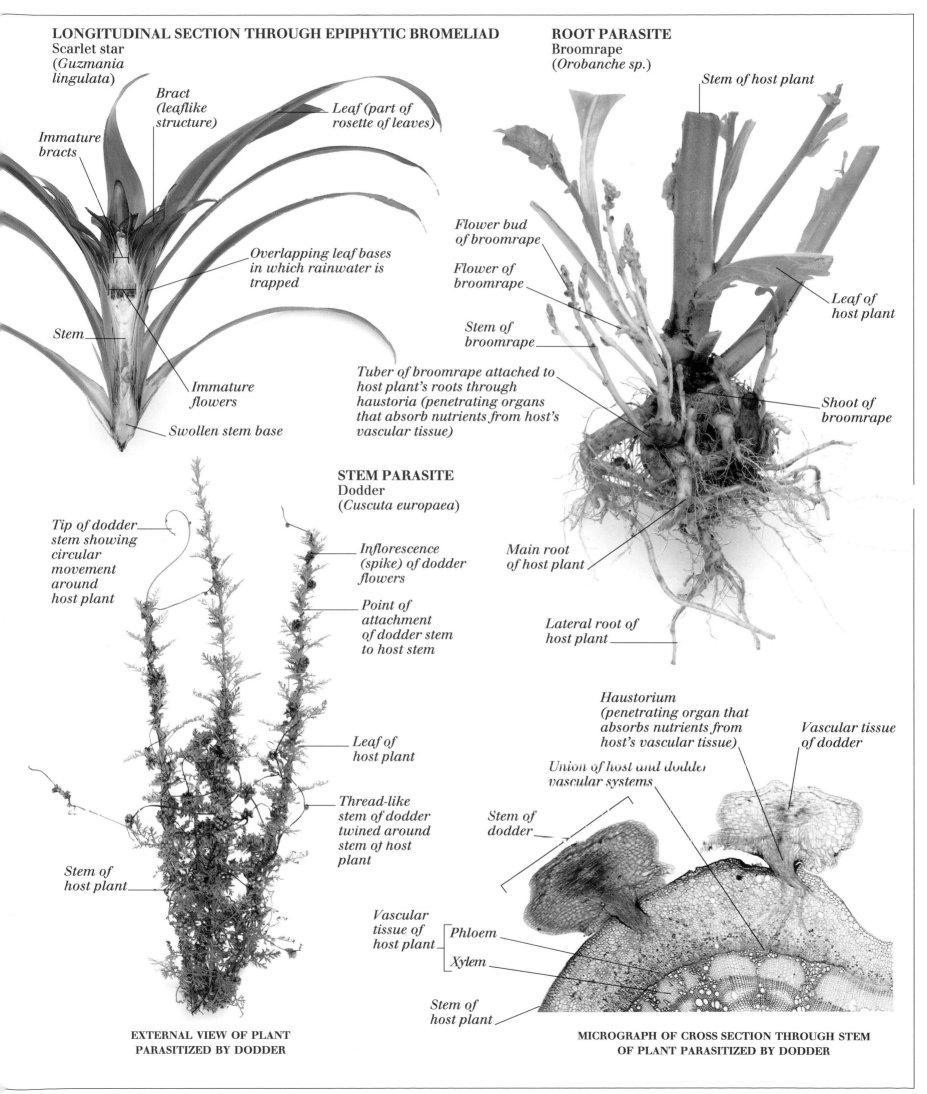

LONGITUDINAL SECTION THROUGH EPIPHYTIC BROMELIAD
Scarlet star
(*Guzmania
lingulata*)

Bract
(leaflike
structure)

Leaf (part of
rosette of leaves)

Immature
bracts

Overlapping leaf bases
in which rainwater is
trapped

Stem

Immature
flowers

Swollen stem base

ROOT PARASITE
Broomrape
(*Orobanche sp.*)

Stem of host plant

Flower bud
of broomrape

Flower of
broomrape

Leaf of
host plant

Stem of
broomrape

Tuber of broomrape attached to
host plant's roots through
haustoria (penetrating organs
that absorb nutrients from host's
vascular tissue)

Shoot of
broomrape

Main root
of host plant

Lateral root of
host plant

STEM PARASITE
Dodder
(*Cuscuta europaea*)

Tip of dodder
stem showing
circular
movement
around
host plant

Inflorescence
(spike) of dodder
flowers

Point of
attachment
of dodder stem
to host stem

Leaf of
host plant

Thread-like
stem of dodder
twined around
stem of host
plant

Stem of
host plant

Haustorium
(penetrating organ that
absorbs nutrients from
host's vascular tissue)

Vascular tissue
of dodder

Union of host and dodder
vascular systems

Stem of
dodder

Vascular
tissue
of host
plant

Phloem

Xylem

Stem of
host plant

**EXTERNAL VIEW OF PLANT
PARASITIZED BY DODDER**

**MICROGRAPH OF CROSS SECTION THROUGH STEM
OF PLANT PARASITIZED BY DODDER**

57

Plant classification

BIOLOGISTS USE A COMMON SYSTEM of classification to catalog the millions of living organisms. Initially, all living organisms are assigned to five large groupings called kingdoms. All plants belong to the kingdom Plantae. The plant kingdom, like other kingdoms, is subdivided into progressively smaller groups, based on the similarities among plants within each group. The plant kingdom is first divided into ten phyla (singular: phylum)—for example, the phylum Angiospermophyta, which includes all flowering plants, such as orchids, palms, cacti, roses, and maples. Each phylum is then subdivided into classes, each class into orders, each order into families, and each family into genera (singular: genus). Finally, each genus is subdivided into species. This system of repeated subdivision produces a "family tree" of all plants. The chart shows the main groups in the plant kingdom. Also included are plantlike organisms: algae (those protists that produce their own food by photosynthesis) and fungi .

KEY
These colors show the classification groupings used in the chart.

PHYLUM

CLASS

FAMILY

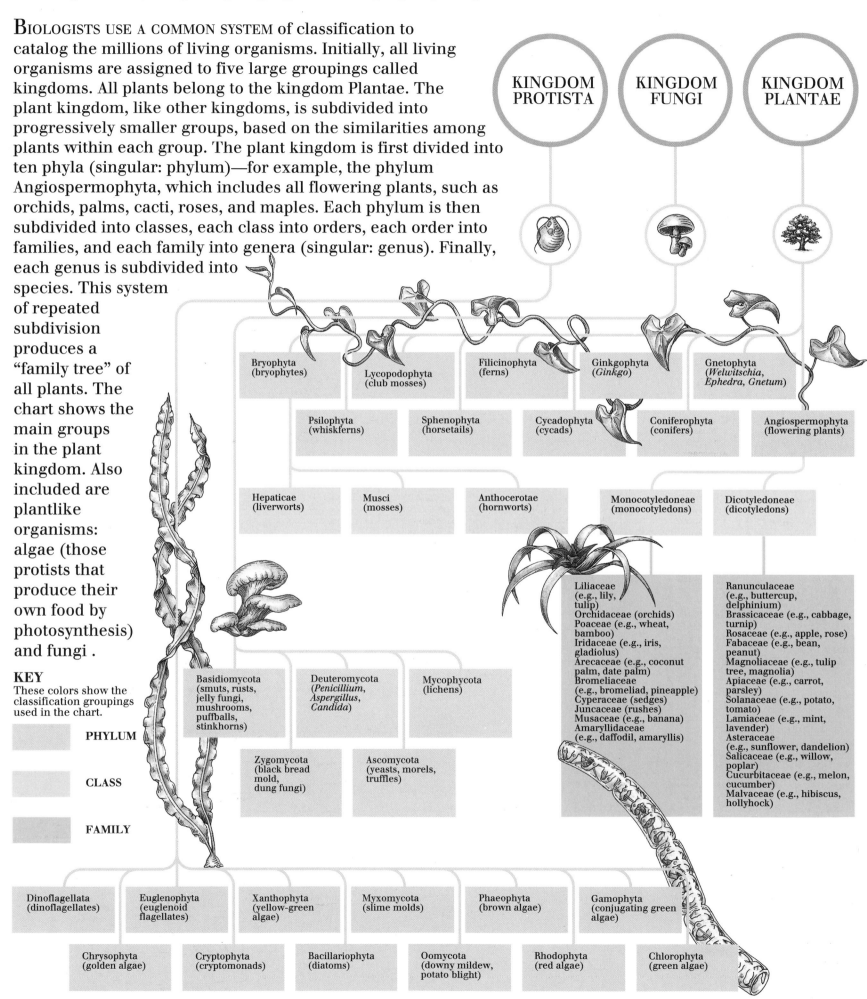

KINGDOM PROTISTA

KINGDOM FUNGI

KINGDOM PLANTAE

Bryophyta (bryophytes)

Lycopodophyta (club mosses)

Filicinophyta (ferns)

Ginkgophyta (*Ginkgo*)

Gnetophyta (*Welwitschia, Ephedra, Gnetum*)

Psilophyta (whiskferns)

Sphenophyta (horsetails)

Cycadophyta (cycads)

Coniferophyta (conifers)

Angiospermophyta (flowering plants)

Hepaticae (liverworts)

Musci (mosses)

Anthocerotae (hornworts)

Monocotyledoneae (monocotyledons)

Dicotyledoneae (dicotyledons)

Liliaceae (e.g., lily, tulip)
Orchidaceae (orchids)
Poaceae (e.g., wheat, bamboo)
Iridaceae (e.g., iris, gladiolus)
Arecaceae (e.g., coconut palm, date palm)
Bromeliaceae (e.g., bromeliad, pineapple)
Cyperaceae (sedges)
Juncaceae (rushes)
Musaceae (e.g., banana)
Amaryllidaceae (e.g., daffodil, amaryllis)

Ranunculaceae (e.g., buttercup, delphinium)
Brassicaceae (e.g., cabbage, turnip)
Rosaceae (e.g., apple, rose)
Fabaceae (e.g., bean, peanut)
Magnoliaceae (e.g., tulip tree, magnolia)
Apiaceae (e.g., carrot, parsley)
Solanaceae (e.g., potato, tomato)
Lamiaceae (e.g., mint, lavender)
Asteraceae (e.g., sunflower, dandelion)
Salicaceae (e.g., willow, poplar)
Cucurbitaceae (e.g., melon, cucumber)
Malvaceae (e.g., hibiscus, hollyhock)

Basidiomycota (smuts, rusts, jelly fungi, mushrooms, puffballs, stinkhorns)

Deuteromycota (*Penicillium, Aspergillus, Candida*)

Mycophycota (lichens)

Zygomycota (black bread mold, dung fungi)

Ascomycota (yeasts, morels, truffles)

Dinoflagellata (dinoflagellates)

Euglenophyta (euglenoid flagellates)

Xanthophyta (yellow-green algae)

Myxomycota (slime molds)

Phaeophyta (brown algae)

Gamophyta (conjugating green algae)

Chrysophyta (golden algae)

Cryptophyta (cryptomonads)

Bacillariophyta (diatoms)

Oomycota (downy mildew, potato blight)

Rhodophyta (red algae)

Chlorophyta (green algae)

Index

Acknowledgments

Dorling Kindersley would like to thank:
Diana Miller for advice and obtaining plant
specimens; Lawrie Springate for dissecting and
identifying specimens, and for advice; Karen Sidwell
for advice; Chris Thody for collecting plant
specimens; Michelle End for advice; Susan Barnes
and Chris Jones at the EMU Unit of the Natural
History Museum for electron micrography; Jenny
Evans at Kew Gardens; Kate Biggs at the Royal

Horticultural Society Gardens, Wisley, Surrey; Spike
Walker of Microworld Services for micrography; Neil
Fletcher for electron micrography and collecting
plant specimens; John Bryant at Bedgebury Pinetum,
Kent; Dean Franklin; Clare Roe; Roy Flooks

Additional editorial assistance:
Fiona Courtenay-Thompson, Danièle Guitton,
Gail Lawther

Additional design assistance:
Sandra Archer, Ellen Woodward

Index:
Indexing Specialists, Hove, East Sussex

Picture credit:
Dr Jeremy Burgess/Science Photo Library:
p.26, top right